Schindler's

Short-Short Stories

&

Uncommon Sense

James A. Schindler

ISBN: 978-0-9818211-0-8

First printing: August 2008-2500 copies

For Information Contact:

James Schindler

1565 E. Tillman Road

Fort Wayne, In 46816

(260) 447-6732

(260) 417-4247 cell

www.jschind34@yahoo.com

Printed by

Craftline Printing

3505 Independence Drive

Fort Wayne, IN 46801-2345

(260) 427-8391

Also by

James A. Schindler

Schindler's Tiny Tales & Whatnot

Acknowledgments

I'd like to thank my wife, Fry, my kids, and my entire family for their loyal support and for patiently listening, in many cases over and over, albeit sometimes reluctantly, to my stories and so forth without complaining too much!

In addition, I'd like to thank my friends, acquaintances, and everyone else who shared their wonderful stories. Special thanks go to Bobby Eshcoff, one of the best storytellers I've ever met.

To my old buddy, old pal Fritz, I say, "Danke schö for your words of wisdom." And to my old Decatur buddies Bob Cook, Sim Hain, Joe Jauregui, Tom "Terrific" Hurst, et al., I say, "Gracias, amigos."

Also, I'd like to extend my heartfelt thanks and gratitude to Eileen Brodmerkel for her help and kind words of encouragement.

Lastly, special thanks go to my daughter, Heidi Rose, for allowing me to include her essay "Go for the Cheese."

In memory of

Joseph E. Schindler

My Big Brother & Hero

1932 - 1999

Common sense and truth don't need

Either art or much display;

Why hunt high-sounding words indeed,

If you have something true to say?

Johann Wolfgang Von Goethe

Faust (as translated by Alice Raphael)

Most people can't rise above themselves! They are

prisoners of their minds, captives of their thinking.

James A. Schindler,

Schindler's Tiny Tales & Whatnot

The world is a looking glass and gives back

to every man the refection of his own face.

William Makepeace Thackeray

Vanity Fair

Short-Short Stories

& Uncommon Sense

That Smells!

I don't know why, but these days for some reason, nobody wants to smell like a human being. Ladies bathe in scented water, use fragrant soap and shampoo, dust intimate parts with sweet-smelling powder, and douse themselves with exotic perfumes so they'll smell like a flower, or a fruit, or anything except a woman.

And most men, not to be outdone by their fair ladies, use fragrant after-shave lotion with an odor like an evergreen tree or some other masculine aroma (whatever that is). In addition, more and more men are using cologne, which is nothing more than a mannish name for perfume. (But what macho man would be caught dead wearing cologne if it were called perfume?)

Furthermore, both sexes gargle with mint-flavored mouthwashes, supposedly making them kissing sweet (assuming, of course, that one wants to kiss a mint). Finally, they apply ample doses of deodorant to parts that have a tendency to sweat; for woe be unto the nose that detects even the faintest odor of perspiration, for it shall run forever!

Quite frankly, I love the natural scent of a woman. If I wanted to smell a flower or some sort of fruit, I'd visit a florist or a fruit stand! Do you really think that any other animal species would prefer the scent of cologne/perfume to that of a potential mate? If not, is it possible that we are being sold odoriferous concoctions to cover up the natural aromas specifically designed by Mother Nature to quicken the pulse, arouse the passions, and attract us to one another? If so, that smells!

A Dirty Crack

It must have been the summer of 1985, when my wife, Fry, and I were driving north on Lafayette, a one-way street in Fort Wayne, Indiana, when a car filled with young men roared by us and then slowed down so we would pass them. After doing this a couple of times, they sped by us again, and as I looked over at the car, wondering what the hell they were up to, the guy in the backseat had his naked butt sticking out the window and was mooning us. When they stopped at the next red light, we pulled beside them and I yelled out the window, "Now that was a dirty crack and ought to be wiped out!"

They howled with laughter and when it died down, the "Mooner" said, as he held a bottle out the window, "Want a beer?"

I guess he didn't mind being the "butt" of my joke!

Good-bye
Companies that don't make money don't make it!

Sick of
My forty-plus years in business has taught me
that a lot of people who call in to work sick
are sick, sick of working!

Wisdom

Never confuse education with wisdom. Education is a learning process by which one gains knowledge. Wisdom is the ability to use knowledge, along with understanding and compassion, to make good decisions that are unencumbered by personal preferences and prejudice. Perhaps the inability to eliminate one's own feelings and intolerances from one's judgments and conclusions is why there are so few truly wise men.

Scotty's Insight

Sir Walter Scott, in his classic tale *Ivanhoe*, asks, and I quote, "Is it just and reasonable to punish one person for the fault of another?"

If he were living in these times, I think that he probably would have written, "Is it just and reasonable to punish one generation for the fault of another?"

Themselves

You can protect people from everything but themselves!

Listen Listen Listen

It pays to listen to everyone, for everyone, in some way, is mentally your superior. There is not a person on earth who doesn't know more about something than you do. So if you listen carefully to each person whom you meet, you might be surprised what you can learn.

Trust Everyone But

I really liked and trusted one of our suppliers for Bandido's Mexican Restaurants. As a result, on just a handshake, he agreed to sell me everything at cost plus 10 percent, and because of that trust, I never checked on him. I have always believed that a man is no better that his word, and in my naïveté , I thought that most men kept theirs.

It was more than ten years later when I finally discovered that he had violated my trust and our agreement by not keeping his word, and had charged me much more than the 10 percent that we had agreed upon. From this experience, I learned that the old sayings "Trust everyone, but cut the cards" and "Trust, but verify" are not only true but, unfortunately, necessary!

The Best Medicine

The best medicine is a cheerful and positive attitude.

Excuse Me But Did I Only Order a Half a Glass?

Maybe it's because I'm from the Midwest, where common sense usually (but not always) reigns, that it bugs me when I order a glass of wine and they bring me a third or a half of a glass. Quite frankly, I don't give a damn what the socially elite in New York or what the "pompous Parisians" think is chic or proper. When I ask for a glass of wine, I want a glass of wine. If I didn't, I would have ordered a half a glass!

A Thousand to None

Losers have a thousand excuses, winners don't need any!

The Bobcat and the Hare

A sick bobcat lay in the grass for several days before he began to feel better. Still too weak to hunt for something to eat, he finally spotted a rabbit.

"Mr. Hare," called the bobcat, "I have been sick and I'm too weak to get up. Would you mind helping me so I can go get something to drink?"

"Oh, no," answered Mr. Hare, "You'll eat me! I know bobcats love to eat rabbits!"

"But, I promise," said the bobcat, "that if you help me, I won't eat you and I will never eat any of your children again."

"Do you really mean it?"

"Cross my heart and hope to die!" swore the bobcat.

"Okay," said Mr. Hare, "but remember, you promised!" and he went over to lend him a hand.

As soon as he tried to help him, the bobcat grabbed Mr. Hare and gobbled him up!

Moral: Desperate creatures are doubly dangerous.

Dedicated to my granddaughter, Dani Ford, who is doubly sweet!

Sue the SOB?

Saturday, I stopped by one of my restaurants, Bandido's, to pick up some chips and salsa to take to the lake. I also got a cup of coffee to go. With the chips and salsa in one hand, the coffee and car keys in the other, I tried to open the car door and spilled the hot coffee all over myself. This made me wonder: Could I sue me?

Without a doubt, if I would have called one of those sleazy, electronic, ambulance-chasing lawyers that advertise on TV, he would have probably said, "Let's sue the SOB. It's his fault!" So I guess that verifies it: I can sue me!

Grim Reaper

If the Grim Reaper wants
me, he isn't going to catch me on the
couch, unless I'm putting it to good use!

Heavenly Hell

If marriages are made in heaven,
why do so many turn out to be pure hell?

A Nickel's Worth

In the 1940s, when I was about five or six years old, my sister Mousie, being a nice person and loving her baby brother, wanted to trade me a dime for a nickel. She kept trying to convince me that the dime was worth more, but I still wouldn't trade with her. After all, in my young mind, I thought that if the nickel was bigger, it must be worth more! Even now, in my late sixties, it still mystifies me why anyone would make the bigger coin worth less.

Waits

He who hesitates, waits!

Polls

How many times have you heard, generally on a TV news program, that the polls show that 60 percent (or whatever the percentage is) of the people are either for or against something? When I hear this, I get the feeling that the media is trying to imply (especially if they concur with the poll) that since most of the people are for it, it must be right.

If the majority of students in a certain class answer the same test question wrong, does that make them right? If not, the consensus that if the majority is for it, it must be right must be wrong!

Moral: The consensus is not always correct and neither are the damn polls!

Senseless

If common sense is not so common,
Why does everybody think they have it?

Smart Customers

Our Bandido's Mexican Restaurant, in Fort Wayne, Indiana, on Winchester Road, is extremely busy. After several weekend nights of standing outside and watching cars circle the building looking for a parking spot and then leaving or parking along the busy road, I decided to build another parking lot. The only site available was a lot across the country road that runs along one side of our restaurant and has practically no traffic.

Naturally, I had to attend a meeting at County Planning to get their approval. During the hearing, I explained that since we didn't have enough parking spaces, customers were parking along the main road, with two wheels off and two wheels on the pavement, creating a safety issue.

I was then asked what provisions I made for people to safely cross the road after they parked in the proposed lot.

"Well," I answered, "I figure if the people are smart enough to eat at Bandido's, they're smart enough to look both ways before crossing the street!"

A Weighty Problem

To get rich, one doesn't need to have a magic potion that will melt the pounds away effortlessly. All one needs is a product that *promises* to! A lot of people are so desperate to lose weight, they don't seem to realize that the only function of many of these products is to shrink the size of their purse not their girth!

The Expensive Meal

My old hometown friend Victor Braun once told me that the most expensive meal he ever had was a blue plate special, back in the 1950s, that cost only $1.99.

"Only $1.99," I repeated. "How could that be the most expensive meal you ever had?"

"It was so damn bad that I took one bite and spit it out. I paid a $1.99 for nothing!"

Ole!

Back in the 1970s, a national Mexican restaurant chain decided to come to Fort Wayne, and they hired John, an inept attorney, to secure economic development bonds for them. Since the bonds are guaranteed up to 90 percent by the government, the banks have little or nothing to lose, which enables them to loan money at a much more favorable rate than a conventional loan. If approved, they would have a distinct advantage over the other local Mexican restaurants, since their cost of doing business would be substantially lower.

Hank Freistroffer, an officer at Bandido's, and I decided to fight the bond approval. As a result, Hank got almost all of the Mexican restaurants owners in town to sign a petition against this unfair scheme.

During the hearing at the city council meeting, the chain's bungling lawyer, John, got up and in his efforts to sway the council, kept emphasizing that they were more than just a Mexican restaurant. This insinuated that the rest of us were somewhat inferior.

Hank then presented to the Council the petition signed by all the local Mexican restaurant owners, and gave a presentation outlining their position.

Next, I explained how unfair approving the bonds would be to the other Mexican restaurant owners who lived, raised their children, and paid taxes in this community for years and years, if not their entire lives.

I concluded by saying, "They've tried to say that they are more than just a Mexican restaurant: They have tacos, we have tacos; they have enchiladas, we have enchiladas; they have burritos, ours are better!"

After the laughter died down, the Economic Development Bonds were denied. *Olé !*

Look'n Up

If you want people to look up to you,

Don't look down on them!

Ted Terrific

Ted Balestreri, the famous restaurateur, once said, "I was a very wealthy kid. My father left me in America, and he left me character. I figure that's about as rich as you want to get."

In addition, he said that his father left him the whole world to make a living in "so I wasn't encumbered!"

With an attitude like that, it's not surprising that Ted is not only a successful businessman, but also, more importantly, a successful human being!

God Bless Ted, and God Bless America!

Denny's Dilemma

It was no more than a minute or two after Ray was served his soup at a Denny's restaurant when he spotted the manager and called him over to his table.

"What can I do for you?" the manager asked.

"I want you to taste this soup."

"Is it cold?"

"No, taste it."

"Is it spoiled?"

"No, just taste the damn soup!" Ray emphatically demanded.

"Okay," the manager reluctantly agreed. Glancing around the table, he asked, "Where's a spoon?"

"Ah-haaaa," Ray said triumphantly as he held up his empty hands.

Where Will You Go?

When you die, I don't believe that
God is going to ask where did you go
to church, or how many times you went?
But I do think that He'll ask what kind of a life
did you lead and how did you treat your fellow man?

Fill'er Up!

In the early 1950s, Decatur, Indiana, a city of five thousand, was a nice quiet little town. There, Tom Hurst's dad, Vernon, not only had a full-time job but he also ran an ornamental-iron business on the side. Hence, at the end of a long hard day, he usually retired early.

Being just shy of sixteen and not having a driver's license, Tom (after he thought his dad had fallen asleep), along with some of his buddies, would silently push his dad's Model A Ford out of the driveway and down the block far enough so his father wouldn't hear it start. Then he and his friends would go for a joy ride around town and when they were done, they would stop a short distance from his house and silently push the car back into the driveway.

These clandestine trips went on for several months until one night, just before he went to bed, Tom's dad said, "Son, if you're going to take the damn car tonight, put some gas in it!"

Improve

You can't improve your life
without first improving yourself!

The Fat in the Hat

I can always tell when I gain weight.
Because when I gain weight,
I have to buy a bigger hat!

Brrrrrrrrrrr

It was so cold this morning, that I didn't see
one brass monkey on anyone's porch!

The Path to Wedded Bliss

If couples treated each other as well after the wedding ceremony

as they did before, marriages would be would be a lot happier

and the love lamp would never grow dim!

The Eyes Have It!

On New Year's Eve many years ago, in my restaurant Jimmie's Pizza, I was told that a very attractive lady in the bar was asking for me. On entering the bar, Hilda, an ex-employee who was dressed to kill in preparation for an evening on the town, ran up and gave me a big hug.

As we stood there chatting, in spite of my best efforts to control them, my hazel eyes kept drifting down to her plunging neckline and ample cleavage. Having a problem with my concentration and feeling like a boob, I, with all the self-discipline that I could muster, raised my peepers and said, "You know, it's really hard for me to look you in the eye with that dress on!"

Too Many Wrongs

"I was wrong once!"

"You were?"

"Yeah, once too many!"

Good Advice from Fritz

Don't give information…gather it!

The Good Germs

It seems to me that there's a current trend to avoid germs at all cost. We disinfect our bathrooms, kitchens, dishes, the air, and who knows what else. We sanitize our hands, other body parts, and gargle with mouthwash to kill germs. Why, some folks avoid as much human contact as possible and won't even shake your hand for fear of getting, God forbid, germs! I think it's safe to say that, if it were possible, some people would purify everything but their minds.

Remember the story of "the Boy in the Bubble"? He was born without an immune system and had to live in a room that was completely germ free, with no human contact, for if he was exposed to any germs, his body wouldn't be able to fight them off and he probably would have died.

Of course, everyone should take prudent measures to maintain reasonable standards of cleanliness and personal hygiene, but in many cases, aren't we going overboard? When we come in contact with most germs, our body destroys them, which in turn strengthens our immune system and its ability to further fight off disease. Thus, these "good germs" actually make us healthier. Even if it were possible to avoid all germs and to live in a sterile environment, wouldn't we then be like "the Boy in the Bubble"?

Not All!

Not all bitches are dogs!

Counselor You're Killing Me!

Fritz, a highly respected attorney and probably the best one I have ever worked with, told me and I quote, "At least fifty percent of all lawyers are incompetent. Why," he went on, "if they were doctors, half of the people would be dead!"

Perhaps that's why Lady Justice is pictured wearing a blindfold. I guess that she just doesn't want to see any more bungling lawyers butchering the law and killing their client's chances for justice!

Parts Go Where?

The problem with most items that we purchase requiring "some assembly" is that the instructions seem to be written by the very engineers who designed them. Hence, the directions are in terms that they understand but are foreign to the average person. Wouldn't it make more sense to have some ordinary people try to put the damn thing together, to make sure the directions are understandable, before they try to sell it?

Even if by chance one is fortunate enough to figure out the lousy instructions, then some of the damn parts will be missing! Could it be because some other frustrated buyer gave the engineers directions (in simple terms, of course) on where to put them?

By George

I honestly think that a great many wives believe that part of their job is to keep their husbands humble. No matter how well he does personally or financially, many a wife is quick to point out any of his weaknesses or faults (real or imagined) that she perceives.

I can just see the president coming home after a hard day of solving the world's problems and his wife saying, "You did what you dumb ass?"

Rumor has it the only reason George became a saint, after a hard day of dragon slaying, was because he didn't have a wife to belittle his accomplishments and cut up his dragon feats with her sharp tongue! Hence, without any wifely character slaying, everyone thought George a saint except the dragon, of course!

He Never Forget His Lunch Bucket!

Back in the 1970s, when I was a drywall contractor, in addition to getting the jobs, I had to make sure that each one was ready and the material was there when my crews showed up, so they could immediately start to work Furthermore, I did all the hiring, purchasing, and actually worked on some of the jobs. Then, in the evenings, I did the bookwork.

One morning as I was driving to work with Joe, one of my employees, my mind was on everything that I needed to do. While wondering if everyone showed up for work, I drove right past the road that I was supposed to turn on. Joe then looked at me and sarcastically commented, "I don't see how anybody can miss their damn turn!"

"Joe," I answered, "if all I had to remember was to bring my lunch bucket to work every day I wouldn't forget it!"

It Hurts!

"Hey Jim, what da'ya think?

"I quit thinking."

"You did?"

"Yeah, it hurts too much!"

Definition

Work: a four-letter word to a lot of people

Anonymous

In Paradise

One Saturday evening, just at dinnertime, I walked into the Paradise Café , an upscale restaurant that I once owned. Noticing that customer service was awful, I approached the manager with these words: "Jerry, what's going on? The service is terrible!"

"I had five waitresses call off tonight," he answered.

"You did?"

"Yeah."

"I suppose all their grandmothers died!" I said sarcastically.

"No," he replied, "only four of them!"

A Car Job

When Andy was sixteen, he asked his dad for a car and Dad replied, "Son, you can have any car you buy." So he got a job!

Paying on Time

I remember back in the nineteen fifties and sixties, when I bought something in Sears or any other store, I would take the items to the cashier and she would ring each item up on a cash register, give me the total, count my change out loud, and thank me. The entire transaction usually took less than a minute.

Nowadays, almost all stores have computerized cash registers that can accumulate a dossier on its customers, track inventory, accept credit/debit cards, simplify record keeping, and provide an endless source of information to the company. The computers do just about everything but run the store.

Every bit of modern technology has been utilized to insure a smooth and efficient operation. Nothing has been overlooked. Nothing, that is, except the customer. Where it used to take less than a minute to check out, one is now lucky if he can get out of there in five to ten minutes, if not longer. Finding the items you need often takes less time than paying for them. Why, I've even been told once that when a department store was extremely busy and the checkout lines were exceptionally long, a young lad outgrew his new clothes before he had a chance to wear them!

Win the Hate

Win the argument and the bastard will hate you forever!

An Eye Opener

We close our eyes when we sneeze.

Sick'O!

About two years ago, sixty-seven-year-old Jim felt awful; he had absolutely no energy and thought that he was on his last leg. After feeling his pulse and noting that it was extremely slow and irregular, his wife, Fry, said, "I'd better take you to the emergency room."

On arriving at the hospital, he was put into a little cubical, where the nurse checked his vital signs while waiting for the doctor. When he finally arrived, the nurse stepped out while the doctor checked Jim over. Upon finishing his exam, the doctor left and in a few minutes the nurse returned.

"What did the doctor say?" she wanted to know.

With a pained expression on his face, Jim replied, "He said I'm gonna die!"

For a few seconds the nurse was overwhelmed with shock and disbelief, until she noticed him smiling, and then somewhat aggravated, she said, "You are sick!"

Later it was decided that Jim needed a heart catheterization, and he was moved to a room to prepare him for the procedure. After inquiring all about his medical history, the nurse started going down a lengthy list, asking him if he was allergic to this or that. Finally she asked, "Are you allergic to latex?"

"I don't know," he quipped, "I never use'em!"

The Big Juan

At Bandido's, Fort Wayne's best Mexican restaurant, we have a huge burrito called "the Big Juan." Jim Bushey, a regular customer, told me that he orders it almost every time he comes in. He likes it so much that his children even bought him a Bandido's "Bite the Big Juan" T-shirt for his birthday. As a matter of fact, Jim said that he has ordered it so often that some of his buddies even call him "the Big Juan."

"Jim," I told him, "if I could get my wife to keep her mouth shut, maybe someone would call me "the Big Juan!"

A Monumental Task

In the 1960s, shortly after I started my own drywall business, I joined an organization made up of young businessmen who, in addition to networking, did community projects. I became a member, thinking that I could not only help the community, but that I could also learn a lot and make a few new friends. At my first meeting, there were approximately twenty members present. After proper introductions were made, the meeting began. The entire session was spent discussing their plans for cleaning the Adams County War Memorial in the Courthouse Square. At the next get-together, again the whole session was dedicated to the same topic. "My god," I said to myself, "give me six men and I can clean the damn monument in less time than you guys spend talking about it!"

I didn't waste any more time going to those meetings and I really don't know if the War Memorial ever was cleaned. But one thing that I do know is "Nothing gets done without the doing!"

Not All!

Early this morning I attended a meeting at the Chamber of Commerce. During the session, Brett, a young attorney, stood up, introduced himself, and began by saying, "I know a lot of you guys hate lawyers."

"Not all of them!" I interrupted!

Definition

A Fool: one who doesn't learn from his/her experiences

A Hard Left!

Why is it that many people who demand their constitutional
right of free speech are outraged when others exercise theirs
and express the opposite view? Perhaps these hypocrites
should be given, in addition to their rights, a hard left!

To Each According to Their Beliefs

If two people truly love each other and want to get married, are they hurting anyone? If not, what difference does their race, religion, or sexual preference make? And, aren't those who oppose such unions simply trying to force others to live by their morals and beliefs?

In an effort to keep everybody reasonably happy, couldn't gay wedding ceremonies, since they are not a traditional marriage between a man and woman, be considered (legal) civil unions?

The Case of the Missing Pickup

Mike, a police officer, drove to Glenbrook, a large shopping mall here in Fort Wayne, to pick up a few things that he needed. After finding what he wanted, he decided to head for home. Returning to the parking lot, he looked and looked for his pickup truck, but couldn't find it anywhere.

Mike assumed that someone had stolen it; not knowing what else to do, he reluctantly called the police. One of his fellow officers, Joe, came out, razzed him a little bit, filled out a missing-vehicle report, and gave him a ride home. Once in his house, he said to his wife, "You won't believe what happened."

"What?" she asked curiously.

"Some [expletive deleted] stole my truck. I had to call the station and Joe came out and brought me home."

"That's strange," his wife said as she opened the kitchen door, thinking that he had driven their car, and peered into the garage. "I just want you to know the pickup's in the garage, but please don't in-CAR-cerate me, I didn't take it!"

Battle of the Gods

Isn't it strange that in all wars that have ever been fought,
both sides have always believed that God was on theirs?

She Never Loses

Jim and Sandi were in Las Vegas on a short vacation. Since they both loved to gamble, they wasted no time. Playing blackjack, Sandi was soon in need of some cash and asked the dealer if he knew her husband, who was gambling at a nearby table.

"Yeah, I know him," he replied.

"Would you be so kind to tell him that I need a few black (one hundred dollar) chips?"

During the next couple of days, Jim was continually giving Sandi cash and chips to keep her occupied at the tables and slots. Finally, as they were heading home, Jim asked, "Honey, how much did you lose?"

"I didn't lose nothing."

"What do you mean you didn't lose nothing, you kept asking me for chips!"

"I didn't lose nothing. I didn't have any money when I came out here, so how could I lose any?"

The Quiet Bells

If only virgins got married

wedding bells would seldom toll!

Exposé

Every time you open your mouth,

your brain is exposed!

Delicate Bottoms

People in glass-bottom boats should tread lightly.

Now *That's* Cold!

"It was so cold last night."

"How cold was it?"

"It was colder than a tax collector's heart

assuming, of course, he or she has one."

The Donkey and the Well

A friend sent me a shorter, simpler version of this
fable on the Internet, by an unknown author, and
I took the liberty of embellishing it.

The Well

More than two thousand years ago, back in olden times, when people needed a reliable supply of water, they dug a hole in the ground, a well. It was usually in the shape of a round circle, several feet across, and it went down twenty, thirty, or more feet, or whatever it took to reach water. After a while, they figured out that if they built a wall about waist high around the well, it would help keep people, animals, dirt, and other debris from falling in and contaminating the water. Later, they decided that if they built a small roof over the well, it would help keep leaves and other debris from blowing into it. In time, a round shaft, with a crank and rope attached, was put between the two posts that supported the roof so folks wouldn't have to lower and raise the water bucket by hand. I'm sure that you have seen pictures of such wells in children's and other books. However, it was in those early days, before the walls were built around the wells, when our tale takes place.

The Tale

Once upon a time, long, long ago, there was a farmer who had a donkey. One day, the farmer couldn't find his ass. He looked high and low and all over the place, but to no avail. He was just about ready to give up when he very faintly heard the sound of his donkey braying. Following the sound, it led him to a well. Now, the farmer looked and looked down the well for the longest time, since he wasn't too smart and could hardly tell his ass from a hole in the ground, but sure enough, he finally saw that his donkey had fallen into it.

The donkey was in a state of panic and was thrashing around and making a lot of noise in the bottom of the well. Even though the farmer thought and thought, he couldn't figure out how to get the donkey out. So he decided to put him out of his misery and just bury him there. He got his friends and neighbors to help him haul in some dirt, and together they started to shovel it down the well.

When the first shovel of dirt hit the donkey, he became hysterical, but as they continued shoveling, a brilliant idea came to him. It dawned on him that every time a shovel of dirt hit his back, he could shake it off and a small mound of soil would build up under him. Then he could step up a little. he did just that. Shovel after shovel, no matter how much it hurt when the dirt struck him, he would shake it off and step up, shake it off and step up. Regardless of how hopeless the situation seemed, the donkey fought on and repeated to himself, "Just shake it off and step up, shake it off and step up!" Finally, after several hours, when it was almost dark, the old donkey, bruised, battered, and exhausted, stepped out of the well.

What seemed likely to bury him actually helped him overcome his adversity.

In real life, it's pretty much the same. Only when we face our problems with a positive can-do attitude and refuse to quit will we be able to overcome them. Then, and only then, will we have learned that the adversities that come to bury us not only give us invaluable experience, but they also make us stronger and wiser.

Moral: When you face adversity, don't try to cover your ass: Just step up and shake it off!

Dedicated to my son John, who,
was never afraid to step up and shake it off!

The Dominant Sex

Since the beginning of time, almost without exception, the male of the species has usually been the fastest and the strongest. Mother Nature gave males superior speed and power so they would be able to protect and to provide for their mates and offspring. As a result, the male was able to rule the roost primarily because of his physical dominance. (This is still apparent in many societies today.)

Being weaker, the female, in order to protect herself and the children from the male's wrath, or to get what she needed, she had to use her charm and wiles. Consequently, after countless generations of using their brains to compensate for the lack of brawn, women have (at least in my opinion) become craftier, more clever, and more cunning and conniving than the male species. They have truly become the dominant sex. Hence, what was once their greatest weakness has evolved into their greatest strength.

If you don't believe this theory, just ask any honest husband who the real boss is!

The Good Lawyer

Everyone hates lawyers until they
need one a good one to save their derriè re!

Good God!

Every major religion has elaborate churches, synagogues, mosques, temples, or other places of worship that were built with the donations and offerings of their members.

These holy monuments not only are expensive to build, but are also costly to operate and maintain, which brings me to the conclusion that there must be a lot of money in God.

Check This

Why is it that a lot of preachers want you to give
the money to God but make the check out to them?
"My preaching ever is, to make them free
in giving pence especially to me."

Geoffrey Chaucer
"The Pardoner's Tale"
The Canterbury Tales

Definition

Beauty is what we're used to!

Smart Advice

If you want people to think
you're smart agree with them!

Wimpy

When eighty-three-year-old Wimpy Rodenbeck heard that his seventy-seven-year-old friend Bobby Eschoff had been in the hospital for a few days but was now home, he gave him a call.

"Bobby, why didn't someone let me know? You could be in Lindenwood [cemetery] and nobody would call me! Nobody tells me nothing!"

After inquiring some more about Bobby's health, Wimpy asked, "Are you doing any exercise?"

"Why?" Bobby wanted to know.

"Because you'll live six months longer in a nursing home!"

No Rules

My daughter Heidi, a junior at the University of Notre Dame, brought Chrissy, her friend and fellow ND cheerleader, home with her for the Easter holiday. As we were making plans to attend Easter Mass, I asked Chrissy if she was Catholic.

"No," she replied. "I'm Methodist. But that's the same as being Catholic with no rules!"

"No kidding," I said. "Can I join?"

A Bullhead

A bullhead: someone who doesn't agree with you!

Name Calling

Never call your spouse a derogatory name,

even in jest, because after a while, what was once

intended to be a joke slowly evolves into something

that is mean, hurtful, and no longer funny.

Sweet Sixteen and Definitely Been Kissed!

Today, my wife, Fry, our friend Sandi Shank, and I were having lunch at Minnie's Diner in Waynedale, when Minnie came over holding a framed picture of an attractive young lady. "Do you know who this is?" she asked.

"That looks like you," Fry said.

"It is. I was sixteen then."

"Sweet sixteen and never been kissed," Sandi chimed in.

"Ha," Minnie chuckled. "Shortly after that picture was taken, I got pregnant!"

The Nutcracker

I met my friend Jim Spangle for lunch today at Bandido's and as we were leaving, he mentioned that this evening he was going to see *The Nutcracker.*

"*The Nutcracker*," I repeated. "Doesn't that make your eyes water?"

Back Home

You can always go back to your ole' hometown,

but it will never again measure up to those wonderful memories!

A Miserable Premise

Did you ever notice that the more miserable

some people are, the happier they seem to be?

The St. Peter Principle

My years as an usher at St. Peter's Catholic Church

have taught me that if you're late and the church

seems packed, there's always room up front!

The Butterfly and the Bee

Once upon a time, long long ago, there was a hardworking honeybee. Every day she would fly back and forth and back and forth, from her beehive to the flower fields, so she could collect nectar to make honey. One day, as she was busy as a bee doing her chores, she saw the most stunning creature she had ever seen. It was black with the most beautiful red, blue, and yellow markings on its wings. As it flew by, it seemed to float lazily in the air with very little effort. It wandered here and there like it had no special place to go or nothing else to do but to enjoy life.

"Oh," said the little bee to herself as she watched the gorgeous butterfly. "I wish I were that beautiful and didn't have to work so hard." Secretly, in her heart, she was a little jealous and would have given anything to be a beautiful butterfly. The next day, as she was collecting nectar in a field of clover, she saw the same beautiful butterfly slowly flying this way and that way, unconcerned about anything in the whole world, when a man came up behind her and caught her in his net. He then put her in a glass jar, screwed the lid on, and went on his merry way, whistling a pretty tune, pleased that he had caught such a fine-looking specimen for his collection.

When the little bee saw this, she never again wanted to be anything other than honeybee, because she knew no one would want to catch her and put her in a jar. Then she thought how lucky she really was since every day, when she was done working, she could go home to her family and friends and have a wonderful meal fit for a queen, or a little bee: lots of delicious honey!

Moral: Count your blessings and just bee yourself!

Dedicated to my granddaughter Elizabeth, who is as beautiful
as the butterfly and as wonderful as the little bee!

Luke Can!

Seven-year-old Luke was scheduled for surgery to correct a congenital defect. When his mother, Holly, teasingly told him that they were also going to remove his "fart and burp button," he had a look of shock and disbelief on his face as he cried out, "Nooooo!"

After his surgery, when the rest of the family found out what Holly had told him, they constantly teased him about his inability to expel wind from either end. At first he believed them, but finally, in sheer desperation to dispel more than the nasty rumor, he ran into the kitchen and yelled, "Mom, Mom, nobody believes me, but I still can! Listen!"

His mom thought he was a gas!

Heaven

"Do you think they have sex in heaven?" she wondered out loud.

"Sure, they do," he answered. "Why do you think they call it heaven?"

The Boob Tube

Did television turn into the boob tube as it
became more risqué , or is that a dumb question?

He Digs It!

In the mid 1950s, Wimpy Rodenbeck and John Eshcoff owned a nice bar and restaurant in downtown Fort Wayne called The Flame.

Nearby was the Palace Theatre, where, in addition to showing the latest movies, they also featured live entertainment.

Because of The Flame's nearness to the Palace, some of the Hollywood stars that performed there, like Eddie Bracken, Gene Autry, Eva Gabor, and Edward Everett Horton and their cast, would frequent that establishment. Now, being astute businessmen with the ability to discern which side their bread was buttered on, Wimpy and John donated a thousand dollars each to the Palace Theatre to help insure its ongoing success.

When one of their friends found about their generous donation, he said, "Wimpy, I didn't know you were a patron of the arts."

"Yeah," Wimp replied, "I dig the culture shit!"

The Age Advantage

One advantage of aging is, it doesn't take long to dry your hair!

What Can I Say?

I hate it when I don't know what I'm talking about.
Because when I don't know what I'm talking about,
I don't know what to say!

A Smart Lesson!

Almost any teacher will tell you
that the smartest kid in the class is not
necessarily the one with the highest grades!

The Final Choice

My son Jimmie played soccer at St. John the Baptist grade school. When he reached the fifth grade, just before the soccer season was about to begin, I got a call from one of St. John's staff members.

"Mr. Schindler?"

"Yes."

"This is St. John's calling and I wondered if you would be interested in coaching our fifth and sixth-grade soccer team?"

"I really don't know anything about soccer. I never played it. I don't even know the rules. When I was a kid, we played kick the can; besides that, I'm almost sixty. You'd better ask one of the younger fathers."

"But, Mr. Schindler, if you don't do it, we can't have a team. We've already asked all the other fathers and they said no!"

Bumpkin

This morning Joe Daniels, Eric Jones, Tim Dirig, and myself had a breakfast meeting at a Bob Evans restaurant. Tim was commenting on the difficulty of doing business with people in New York City and on the East Coast.

"Why's that?" I asked.

"Because they think anyone from Indiana's a 'bumpkin.'

"A bumpkin?" I repeated. "Why would they think that? They don't even know me!"

Keep it Moving!

The human body, as it ages, is a lot like an old car with a lot of miles. Every once in a while, a part has to be repaired or replaced. When that happens, just fix it and go on down the road. After all, it's a lot harder for the Grim Reaper to catch you if you're moving!

You Can't Miss!

You can't miss what you never had!

Expertless

We all know people who think they're experts
on things they know nothing about!

How Old Would You Be?

Someone once asked me, "How old would you be,
if you didn't know how old you were?"
"I don't know," I replied, "my body tells me
I'm no kid, but my brain disagrees!"

Word Watch

If we'd watch our words,
we'd eliminate a lot of our worries.

The Wannabe

We've all seen people who like to rub shoulders with the rich and famous and also act like they are, too. These folks are called "wannabes." The following poem is dedicated to those fools who spend their lives wanting to be someone or something that they don't have the talent or drive to be.

Wannabe

(Sing to the tune of "Look at Me, I'm Sandra Dee," from the play *Grease*.

Look at me, the Wannabe,

Oozing with vast vanity.

You won't see my face,

In just any old place

I'm me the Wannabe!

Look at me, the Wannabe,

Where it's not ritzy,

You'll never find me.

I only dine with folks that are fine,

I'm me the Wannabe!

Look at me, the Wannabe,

With movers and shakers,

That's where you'll find me.

I'd love to be one, but I can't get it done.

I'm me, the Wannabe!

Would He Feed You a Kroc?

(As I imagined it)

In 1968, McDonald's opened their one thousandth hamburger unit and was without a doubt the most successful restaurant chain in the world. A clever young reporter became aware of this and decided to interview the owner and CEO, Ray Kroc. He wanted to find out, and do an article on, what made McDonald's so successful. An appointment was set up and he was ushered into Mr. Kroc's impressive office.

After the introductions and niceties were dispensed with, the reporter said, "Mr. Kroc, in a few short years you've built the largest and most successful restaurant chain in the world. How did you do it? What's your secret?"

"Well," Mr. Kroc said, "there really are no secrets in the restaurant business, but if you want to know what made McDonald's successful, I'd have to say that it's QSC."

"QSC?" the reporter repeated. "What's that?"

"Quality, service, cleanliness. QSC."

"That's it?" the reporter questioned.

"Yes," Mr. Kroc went on. "If you serve quality food, give good service fast, and keep the place squeaky clean, you can't miss!"

The reporter, expecting a more complicated formula, was surprised at the simplicity of QSC. Instantly, he could see the logic of it and was completely convinced that he had just been given the secret of success by the captain of the restaurant industry.

As quickly as he could, he rushed out of Mr. Kroc's office and informed the world of McDonald's formula. From that time forth, everyone in the restaurant business, whenever the subject came up, nodded their heads in infinite wisdom and said, "If you want to be successful, you have to have QSC."

Now, Ray was no dummy. He had only told the reporter half of the story. While everyone else was running around extolling QSC, McDonald's kept implementing QSC plus VHO. VHO stands for value, hospitality, and other factors. Value is giving as much as you can at the lowest possible price. Hospitality, plain and simple, is just being nice to your customers and making them feel at home. Other factors are the many things that must be just so, to help insure a restaurant's success. It could be chair design, lighting levels, background music, store temperature, etc.

For example, if a restaurant played blaring hard rock or rap music, I'm sure quite a few customers would make a hasty departure. There is a restaurant that my wife won't go to in the summer because it is so cold. Are the chairs comfortable? All of these things and many others affect the dining experience.

Ray Kroc, the old fox, knew this. He also knew that if you throw the wolves a bone, you can keep them busy while you distance yourself from the pack. So, while his competitors were occupied (with the bone he threw them) and running around saying you gotta have QSC, McDonald's quietly implemented QSCVHO, the whole program. It was years before many of his rivals figured out the rest of his recipe for success. Why, even today, when you eat out, I'm sure you've noticed that many of them still haven't!

Club-less

Many years ago, a friend asked me if I would like to join one of the country clubs here in Fort Wayne.

"This kind of reminds me of a story that someone once told me about Groucho Marx," I said, and I proceeded to tell it to him.

In the early 1900s, many of the more exclusive country clubs in New York would not let Jews join. Groucho, a well-known comedian and movie star during that time, was Jewish. However, over the past few years, he had become so famous that the membership committee of one of those prestigious country clubs decided that it would enhance their status if they had Groucho as a member. As a result, one of the members was instructed to contact Groucho and ask him if he would care to join their organization.

A meeting was arranged at one of New York's trendiest spots and during lunch, when the famous comedian was asked if he would like to join their club, he replied, "What! Any club that would have me for a member I don't want no part of."

No Regrets

I would rather try and fail than
never try and regret it for the rest of my days;
for one seldom laments actions that are appropriately taken

He's Not that Smart

Why is it when a husband explains something to his wife, she doesn't think he knows what he's talking about? But when a friend or stranger tells her the exact same thing, she believes it like it was the gospel truth! Could the reason possibly be that there's something in her subconscious that tells her her husband can't be that smart, if he married her?

Continuing Education

Unfortunately, many students believe that graduation is the end of their education. However, the reason that the graduation ceremony is called a commencement is because the term "commence" means to begin. Thus, this implies that one's graduation should be the beginning of a life long learning process.

A formal education is what one learns in school. An informal education is what one learns through ongoing self-study, personal improvement, and experience. However, the lack of a *formal* education does not necessarily mean that one is ignorant. There are too many examples of great men, Abraham Lincoln, Henry Ford, and Thomas Edison, to name a few who had very little formal schooling yet were obviously well educated.

Finally, I think it is apparent that a good formal education will get you into the game of life, but your continuing self-education is what will make you a winner.

Moral: School should never be out!

Young Mind

One Saturday morning, my nephew, John (JJ) and I were cutting up a tree in my backyard. After a couple of hours of running the chain saw, I sat down and took a break.

"I don't know what's the matter with me," I said, "but I'm really pooped!"

"The trouble with you, Uncle Jimmie," JJ noted, "is that you have a thirty-year-old's mind in a seventy-year-old's body!" Which goes to prove that the old biblical saying "the spirit is willing but the flesh is weak" is definitely true. (In case of doubt, just ask my wife!)

Skill or Luck?

Did you ever notice winners believe cards

is a game of skill, while losers think it's luck?

The Imperial Salad

Recently my wife, Fry, and I were in a local restaurant and after I finished ordering my dinner, the waitress asked, "Would you like a salad with that?"

"What kind do you have?"

"We have a tossed salad, a taco salad, Caesar salad, and…"

"Is that Caesar salad Julius or Augustus?" I interrupted.

"Gee, I don't know. I'll go ask the chef."

(No, she wasn't blond!)

Their Worst Nightmare

I can't remember how many people have told me that when they retire, their dream is to open a nice little restaurant or bar. "Be careful," I caution them. "You'd better be committed, do your homework, and expect to work longer and harder than you have ever worked in your life, because that's what it's going to take for you to be successful. If you're not willing to do that, your lifelong dream might just turn into your worst nightmare!

Silver-tongued

The silver-tongue gets the gold!

Too much of a good thing can be wonderful!

Mae West

Not Quite!

Shirley, a widow with seven children, met Bob, and after dating for a year or so, they decided to get married. A short time after the wedding, one of Shirley's old friends called and, during the course of their conversation, asked if Bob had any kids.

"He has two and a set of twins," Shirley answered.

"Twins?

"Yeah, a boy and a girl," Shirley replied.

"Are they identical?"

Sickening!

Being sick is sickening!

The Advantage of Poverty

Jerry Henry, a very successful entrepreneur here in Fort Wayne, was the oldest of seventeen children and grew up in an extremely poor family. Today he not only owns several thriving businesses and rental properties, he is also one of the most honest and forthright businessmen in northern Indiana.

Just this evening Jerry was telling me about his son, Pete, who recently graduated from business school. When I asked him if his son was going to be an entrepreneur like his dad, he answered, "I don't know. I think our environment shapes us, and I had the advantage of poverty."

If more people had Jerry's attitude and used their disadvantaged childhood as a reason to excel instead of an excuse to fail, they too would realize that their poverty-stricken youth was indeed "an advantage"!

Shooting from the Lip

Did you ever wonder why the opponents of our constitutional right to bear arms, keep shooting off their mouths?

The Beat Goes On

A happy heart never misses a beat!

It Lies!

At the local YMCA, after I work out, I always weigh myself. Today when I went over to their huge Toledo scale to do just that, a rather rotund gentleman, with a look of frustration on his face, was just stepping off of it. As I started to weigh myself, he looked at me and blurted out, "Don't believe it, it lies!"

Schindler's First Rule of Law

Avoid lawyers!

The Greatest Joy

One of the greatest joys in life
is when your children make you proud!

Severin Schurger (1909 - 1993)

Severin Schurger was an attorney and
a mentor of mine, during my youth. More
importantly, he was one of the most honorable
individuals I have ever met and an exception to
Schindler's First Rule of Law. Severin once gave me
some sound advice when he said, "Never get into an argument
with anyone who buys ink by the barrel and paper by the carload."

Definition

Automatic dishwasher: a storage facility for dirty dishes

No Passing Allowed

The best thing about being in last place is…

no one's ever going to pass you!

Judge BoBo

Judge Bobo, a deeply religious man who was well versed in the Bible, was aware that in the Old Testament, Joshua made the sun stand still.

Back during Prohibition, the good judge presided over a court in Decatur, Indiana, and one day a black man, by the name of Joshua, was hauled before him for bootlegging.

"Joshua," the good-natured judge asked, "are you the one who made the sun stand?"

"No sir, Mr. Judge, ah's duh one dat made da moonshine!"

The Big Hit

If you've fixed it and it still won't work, get a bigger hammer!

We All Love Dead Presidents

Brian wanted to buy his mother, who just loved diamonds, something nice, so he went to the local coin and jewelry shop. The proprietor, who purchased his wares from individuals, estates, and so forth, had a real nice line of rings, necklaces, bracelets, and other jewelry.

Brian finally found a diamond ring that he thought his mother would like, and tried to pay by check, but the jeweler said," I don't take checks; bring me some dead presidents."

Having no idea what he meant, and too embarrassed to ask, Brian went home and asked his mother. "Oh," she informed him, "he wants cash. You know bills with dead presidents on them."

Did the jeweler want dead presidents to avoid taxes, or did he want them because now they don't stink like some did when they were alive?

More than One

Many many years ago, when the world was comprised mostly of farms and small communities, the dumbest or goofiest person living in each village was referred to as "the village idiot" and it was commonly thought that every village had one.

Today, many folks believe that most communities have a lot more than one! What do you think? Or is that an idiotic question?

Do It Now!

Do it now! For tasks put off seldom get easier!

No Drive

Prior to World War II, it was fairly common in many small Midwestern towns that a lot of families didn't own cars and therefore many folks never learned to drive.

After World War II started, in the early 1940s, Sim Hain, a small-town boy from Decatur, Indiana, found himself flying one of the huge, four-engine, B24 bombers on missions over the South Pacific. Sim flew forty-five missions and had more than a thousand hours of flying time. Consequently, he was a well-seasoned combat pilot.

One particular morning Sim was supposed pick up the commanding officer (CO) and drive him to his office. After checking out a staff car from the motor pool, Sim showed up at the CO's quarters with not only a car, but also a driver. When the CO asked him why he brought a driver along, Sim, a little red-faced from embarrassment, explained, "Sir, I never learned how to drive!"

You Name It!

In the Catholic religion, the Sacrament of Confession is the act confessing one's sins. The procedure is that one tells the Confessor (priest) his sins and how many times he committed each one. Then the priest, in the name of God, absolves (forgives) him and gives the sinner a penance, usually some prayers to say.

Just the other day one of my Catholic friends asked me if I still went to confession. "Sure," I replied. "I just tell the priest, 'You name it, and I'll tell you how many times'!"

Suck Ups?

Are people who drink through straws suck ups?

Six Times!

Usually, at the age of six, Catholic children make their first confession. As the time drew near, Kotzie, a typical six-year-old, was worried because she didn't have any sins to confess. She knew she had to tell the priest something, so when her time came, she began by saying, "Bless me, Father, for I have sinned. I committed adultery six times!"

Laps around the Beads

Frank attended a Catholic school and, along with his classmates, was required to go to confession every Friday. As penance for their sins, they were required to say some prayers. How many times each prayer was to be said depended on the severity and frequency of their transgressions. Obviously, the more serious the sins and the more times they were committed, the more prayers they were required to say.

In the Roman Catholic faith, simply put, the rosary is a circle of beads on a string that is used to count prayers, so Frank and his pals referred to their penance as laps around the beads. Frank, being a high-spirited, lusty lad, usually got a lot of laps and, over time, by the process of elimination, he learned which sins got the most laps.

Once, after he left the confessional, while kneeling in church saying his penance, he noticed there were a few girls who were also doing a lot of laps and he decided that they would be the fun ones to date. Overjoyed at his discovery but unable to keep it to himself, he foolishly told his friends. Thereafter, every Friday, Frank and his buddies sat in back of church taking note of which girls were doing the most laps and those were the ones they asked out.

One Friday, a nun noticed all the boys sitting in the back row and asked Frank what they were doing. Being young, and believing that he would go straight to hell if he lied to a nun, he confessed. After she whomped him good (as a penance, of course), his body then felt the wrath of God as administered through his mother. On returning home, Frank's father again gave him what for.

Learning his lesson well, Frank never again sat in the back row of the church. First, he didn't like the whup'ns, and secondly, by now he already knew the girls who did a lot of laps!

The Droopsies

Vicious rumors have it that
the 1960s, Ban the Bra Brigade
is now suffering from the droopsies.

Bob's Knows

During World War II, Bob Heller, an insurance agent from Decatur, Indiana, was speaker of the Indiana House of Representatives. Over years of enduring the ins and outs of politics, he learned his lessons well, and wisely commented, "In politics, no matter how it looks that's not the way it is!"

Definition:

Miser: Anyone who's tighter than an old pair of pants on a fat lady!

The Only Jinx

The only jinx is negative thinking.

Your thoughts are like a magnet. If you think

positive thoughts, you attract the positive. If you

think negative thoughts, you attract the negative. Hence, either

you accentuate the positive or suffer the negative. The choice is yours.

Worry

It's not what your kids tell you, it's

what they don't tell you that you should worry about!

Bob Sweigert

Go for the Cheese

(An essay, written to submit with my application for

admission to the University of Notre Dame)

By

Heidi Rose Schindler

December 22, 2000

Recently, my father bought the book entitled *Who Moved My Cheese?* by, Dr. Spencer Johnson, and asked me to read it. I decided to do as he asked; first, because it was pretty short, and second, because Dad said he learned a good lesson from it that he wished he had known when he was my age. Little did I realize the profound impact that it would have on me!

The story is about two little mice, Sniff and Scurry, and two tiny men, Hem and Haw, who were about the size of the mice. They all lived in a dark and foreboding labyrinth. Every morning they would get up, put on their sneakers, leave their cozy room, and run through the halls in this maze looking for the cheese that sustained them. Usually they could find bits and pieces scattered in the halls. They tried many passages and the rooms they led to, but they were always empty. One day, at the end of a particular scary corridor, they entered a room and, lo and behold, it was filled with all kinds of cheese. There was Cheddar, Limburger, Colby, Swiss, and lots of the other favorites of mice and men. Why, there was even American! Now they could all enjoy their favorite kinds, and from that time on they no longer had to roam the sinister passageways. Each morning they would arise and go straight to the room filled with cheese and feast until they could feast no more.

One day, when they entered that room, the cheese was all gone. As soon as it was apparent that there was no more cheese, Sniff and Scurry ran off down the halls and into the maze, following their noses looking for more. In no time they found another room piled high with it.

Meanwhile, Hem said, "Who took our cheese?" It isn't fair! It's our cheese!" Haw wanted to go look for some more, but he was afraid to enter the labyrinth alone, with its dark and scary corridors. Each day they grew weaker, and finally Haw thought, *What would I do if I wasn't afraid? Why, I'd go looking for more cheese!* He tried to talk Hem into going with him, but Hem wouldn't listen. Hem said he was going to stay right where he was, until someone brought back his cheese. Finally, Haw, weak and afraid, left on his own and, after wandering through the dark passages for some time, entered the room where Sniff and Scurry were stuffing themselves with the most delightful cheeses.

After I finished the book, I discussed it with my dad and he told me this story, which reminded me of Hem. He said that he loves Notre Dame because in the 1940s, their football players would come to St. Vincent's Villa, the orphanage where he lived, to visit the kids. "They were our heroes!" he told me. Then, with tears in his eyes, he said that he was afraid to apply to Notre Dame. "I didn't think that I was good enough. After all, I was a kid from a broken family who was raised in an orphanage and then lived on charity in a foster home. I thought, *They wouldn't want me!*

I was a little bit like Dad and Haw. I was reluctant to send my application to Notre Dame because I was afraid. I knew that I could easily get into many other colleges, but I was afraid that I wasn't good enough to be accepted at Notre Dame. Maybe my grades, my class standing, or my test scores weren't high enough. Worst of all, I was afraid that I would be rejected. Then, I remembered what Haw said: "What would I do if I wasn't afraid?" The answer was clear: I would apply to Notre Dame and hopefully fulfill my life's dream.

Thanks to Dad, and to Sniff, Scurry, Hem, and Haw, who taught me "What would I do if I wasn't afraid?" I got the courage to send in my application and go for the cheese!

Author's note: Heidi is now a senior and captain of the
varsity cheerleaders at the University of Notre Dame.

52

The Headstone

Sal, an Italian immigrant and master stonemason, worked many years on the National Cathedral, in Washington, D.C. Over time he became so fond of that structure that when his wife was on her deathbed, he asked for permission to have her buried there. He was told no, because one must be either famous or some sort of a dignitary to be interred there.

So upon his wife's death, Sal had her cremated and he secretly had her ashes mixed into the mortar that he used to lay some of the stone on that imposing structure. And still, to this very day, nary a person can tell which one is her headstone!

Is Minimus Maximus?

Mark is a good friend of mine, and his last name, Klein, is German for small or little. Mark stands about five foot five, so his name is very befitting. However, if we were to measure his character, his integrity, and his heart, he'd be a giant of a man!

Several years ago I teasingly started calling him Marcus Maximus ("Big Mark"), obviously playing off of his minimus height. And every time I called him Marcus Maximus, he would just beam. Why, even to this very day, when I call him that, it brings a big smile to his face. Is it possible that he knows something we don't know, and could he really be Marcus Maximus?

The Money Flee

Money unattended…has a

mysterious way of disappearing!

He Luvs'em

A few weeks ago I had breakfast with my friends of many years: Bob Cook, and JoJo Jauregui, who is of Mexican heritage. After we finished eating, Ed Sprunger sat down in the booth beside Bob and joined us.

Sometime during the ensuing conversation, Ed mentioned that he had never been to Bandido's, one of our Mexican restaurants. Being somewhat of a logical thinker, I asked the obvious question: "Why not?"

"I don't like Mexican food."

Sliding over in the booth next to JoJo, I put my arm around him, looked at Ed, and said, "But you like Mexicans, don't you?"

Let's Face It

At a recent wedding, my wife, Fry, and I ran into Sherry Chapin, an old friend. Somehow, during the course of the conversation, the subject of age came up.

"Do you know how old Jimmie is?" my wife asked Sherry.

"He's about my husband's age," she replied, "Fifty-seven, fifty-eight."

"He'll be seventy next month."

"Oh my god, I can't believe it!" she said, as she looked me over. "I thought he was about Chet's [her fifty-five-year old husband] age." Then, staring intently at my face, she blurted out, "You had a face-lift!"

"Sherry," I said, "if I'd had a face-lift, do you think I'd look like this?"

Hell? No!

Assuming God is our heavenly Father and we are truly God's children whom He loves infinitely more than we love our own, then it is unthinkable that he would punish any of His children, no matter what their sins, with eternal damnation. That is, to condemn them forever and ever, to burn in hell.

I think that most of us would agree that eternal damnation is not a just punishment, no matter what the sin. Therefore, considering that God is more just and more forgiving than man will ever be, it is virtually impossible for me to believe that He would condemn his children to such a fate.

If this premise is true, then could it be that the Devil and his fiery netherworld are the creation of some clever cleric's fertile imagination, designed to scare the hell out of his flock to make them behave? After all, the fear of hell has been known to scare "the Devil" out of a lot of people!

The Pits

Recently, my son-in-law, Eric Jones, and I took a business trip to Tulsa, Oklahoma. Since our goal was not to make Mr. Hilton rich, we stayed in the same hotel room. After showering, I discovered that I had forgotten to pack my deodorant. "Eric," I yelled from the bathroom, "if you let me borrow your underarm deodorant, I promise I won't use it on my leg pits!"

Hesitation

He who hesitates is bossed!

Entitlement

Kenny walked into the diner, sat in the only empty seat at the counter, and ordered a cup of coffee. Next to him sat a well-groomed, silvered-haired gentleman. Noticing Kenny's dejected look, he said, "I don't know what's the matter, son, but nothing could be that bad."

"Easy for you to say. I just got laid off recently. I have a two-month-old baby, my wife's sick, and I don't know what the hell I'm going to do! I've been looking for a job and can't find a damn thing. I'm getting desperate!"

"Sometimes when things look the worst is when they start to get better. "You can't give up. You've got to keep on trying. Your family is counting on you," the old gentleman pointed out. "I'll tell you what, meet me here tomorrow morning and maybe I can help."

The next morning the two met and after inquiring more about Kenny's circumstance, the old guy gave him an envelope. Kenny opened it and pulled out two crisp hundred dollar bills. Surprised, Kenny asked, "What's this for?"

"Just something to help tide you over until you get on your feet."

"I don't know when I'll be able to pay you back."

"Don't worry about it," the old man said. "Can you meet me here next Monday morning?"

"Sure," Kenny replied. "What else have I got to do?"

Every Monday morning the two met at the diner and the old guy gave Kenny an envelope with two hundred-dollar bills in it. This went on for more than a year. Finally, one Monday, the old gent handed Kenny an envelope and upon opening it, he found only a single hundred-dollar bill.

With a long face, Kenny looked at his benefactor and said, "What's the matter? You only gave me a hundred dollars!"

Moral: When a person gets a handout or something for nothing, after a while, at least in his or her mind, it becomes an entitlement.

The Porcupine and the Pups

Once upon a time, a hungry fox and her pups were hunting for something to eat when they spotted a porcupine. The pups, being very rambunctious, took off after the porcupine even though their mother yelled and yelled for them to come back. Expecting an easy meal, the pups tore in to their prey and soon found out that the only thing they had for their efforts was a mouth full of barbed quills. Yelping and howling from pain, they ran back to their mother, who had an awful time pulling the quills out. After that, as long as the pups lived, no matter how hungry they were, they never again wanted porcupine for dinner!

Moral: Experience is the best but the most painful teacher.

Also: Listen to your mother!

Dedicated to my sweet granddaughter, Reilly Shull,
who always listens to her mother!

Dumbest

The dumbest answer to any question has to be,
"Because that's the way we've always done it!"

Political Payoffs

The problem with the United States, and our form of government, is that for the most part, the majority of people vote for the candidates who promise to give them the most goodies, at the taxpayers' expense, of course. Unscrupulous politicians who will do anything to get elected promise their constituents all kinds of handouts and benefits even if it is not in the best interest of the general welfare.

Alexander Tyle, (a Scottish history professor, who lived if the 1700s,) said, "A democracy is always temporary in nature; it simply cannot exist as a permanent form of government. A democracy will continue to exist up until the time that voters discover that they can vote themselves generous gifts from the public treasury. From that moment on, the majority always votes for the candidates who promise the most benefits from the public treasury, with the result that every democracy will finally collapse due to loose fiscal policy, [which is] always followed by a dictatorship."

When a politician promises their constituents all kinds of goodies and benefits for their votes, isn't that the same as bribery? In other words, vote for me and I'll see that you get this or that. If that isn't a form of buying votes, what would you call it? After all, does it really matter if the payoff is before or after the election?

Quoting Lary

Contradictory Terms: Military-intelligence

Lary

Headache

"Honey?"

"Not tonight, I've got a headache!"

"Don't you remember that old saying?"

"What in the world are you talking about?"

"If you don't use it, you'll lose it!"

A Positive Light

Are people who call red lights, green lights more

positive than people who call green lights, red lights?

If so, do really positive people call stoplights go lights?

The Skinny on the Fat

I think it is obvious to every rational adult that if you take in more calories, which are nothing more than fuel (energy) for the body, than you use, you're going to gain weight. Why? Because excess calories that are not used for normal bodily functions and maintenance are stored as fat. To my knowledge, there is no medical doctor or scientist in the world who will dispute this fact. Hence, the science of losing weight is not really that complicated. Simply put, if you routinely eat more calories than you use, you're going to get fat! So, if you want to lose weight, all you have to do is to remember the old saying "If you don't put it in, you won't put it on!"

Now *That's* Tight

Why do the fattest women wear the tightest pants?

Schindler's Guaranteed Weight-Loss Program

There are only two guaranteed ways to lose weight.

First, push yourself away from the table,

and secondly, get off your ass!

They Auto Go!

Doug is one of the most talented guys who ever worked for us at Bandido's. He not only wrote and filmed many of our commercials, he has also composed the music and words to the ever-popular "You deserve a night out at Bandido's." Currently, he is developing new recipes in addition to improving some of Bandido's old ones.

Today, he called and told me that he would be out of town for a few days.

"Where ya going?" I asked.

"To New Orleans."

"New Orleans?"

"Yeah, they're having Southern Decadence."

"Southern Decadence," I parroted him again. "What's that?"

"It's kind of like a Mardi Gras for gays."

"You're kidding!"

"No," he answered. "There'll be over two hundred thousand gay guys there."

"Wow," I exclaimed. "Will there be any lesbians?"

"No," he replied, "they'll be home, working on their cars!"

Get a Job!

Francis's father and mother were first-generation immigrants. His father was from Germany, his mother from Italy, and both spoke broken English. Like many first-generation Americans, they encouraged their children to work hard and to get a good education. Francis not only did that, but he also went on to get a PhD in psychology and now has a nice private practice.

After many conversations about his practice with his immigrant parents, one day his mother said to him, "Francis, all-a you do is-a practice, practice! When a-you gonna quit da practice and getta nice-a job?"

Another time, when his mother was visiting his office, a patient who was just leaving, shouted "Good-bye, Doc." On hearing this, she asked, "What's-a he calling you a Doc for? You name is Francis. I baptized you Francis! Why donna he call-a you by you name?"

Cribbing

On a recent Las Vegas trip, as my wife, Fry, and I were going down for breakfast in the elevator, there was a clean-cut man with a goatee. "Going to the psychologist convention?" I inquired.

"No," he replied. "To the baby furniture convention."

"With your goatee and appearance, I thought you looked like you might be going to the psychologist convention, at the Stardust [hotel and casino]."

"Psychologist? Oh, you mean like Sigmund [Freud]," he said. "I thought you were ribbing me."

"No," I answered, "I was cribbing you!"

Political Incorrectness

In a recent case, the United States Supreme Court ruled against a white University of Michigan student who claimed she was discriminated against because she was refused admission to their law school while others, with lower qualifications, were admitted solely because of their ethnicity. Certainly the Justices had to be aware that this was a classic case of reverse discrimination.

I think it is fair to assume that every just and reasonable person would agree that discrimination, in any form, is wrong. If so, how in heaven's name can anyone, much less the United States Supreme Court, justify reverse discrimination? This decision, which is obviously a miscarriage of justice, had to been made in the name of "political correctness," which, in many cases, is nothing more than a means to circumvent real justice. This ruling does, however, verify that the Supreme Court Justices are as human as the rest of us and suffer from the same weaknesses that afflict most of mankind. That is to say, their decisions can be, and many times are, influenced by their emotions, beliefs, prejudices, and what is currently viewed as being politically correct. Unfortunately, this travesty of justice not only serves to diminish the Court's reputation in the eyes of many Americans, but also in the rest of the world!

Moral: Man-made justice is not always just!

The Good Sinner

Lary and Joey Lee were typical counterculture children of the 1960s. For many years they did everything that was popular during those turbulent times, which included all kinds of drugs and practically every other vice, legal or illegal.

Recently I was having a couple of beers with Lary, who has since given up drugs, and he told me that Joey Lee had also quit all drugs, including alcohol. "He's a preacher now, just like his daddy," Lary informed me. "Joey Lee told me that he wanted to be just as good a Christian as he was a sinner. Why," he went on, "if I ever decide to go to church, I'd go to his."

"How come?" I asked, somewhat puzzled.

"Because he has to be a damn good preacher, cause he sure was a good sinner!"

Cuz

Cuz was from the Deep South, at least second or third-generation inbred. He couldn't read or write a lick, and was about as sharp as a shoulder blade. Recently, he started to date his mother's best friend, who was also his old babysitter, and now they're shack'n up together.

He was also seeing his first cousin on the side and when he learned that his babysitter-girlfriend found out, he knew that he was in deep poop, so he stopped at the local watering hole to have a drink and figure out what he was gonna do.

While he was having a beer, his buddy Lary noticed his worried look and said, "Cuz, I haven't seen you this nervous since your sister got pregnant."

"Don't blame that on me," Cuz said, shaking his head. "Ah never could catch her!"

No Sympathy

In the 1970s, Joe, the founder and president of a large pizza chain with more than four hundred stores, was the center of attention at one of their social functions. Surrounded by a group of fawning admirers, Joe was explaining that the cast on his arm was the result of falling down on his yacht. As he was beaming and basking in all that attention, while his groveling admirers bewailed the terrible tragedy that befell him, I finally spoke up and said, "Joe, I find it pretty hard to have much sympathy for anyone who broke their arm falling down on their damn yacht!"

A Goner!

Today I ran into my son's parked car as I was backing out of the drive. "What's the matter with you?" my wife, somewhat annoyed, asked. "I don't know," I replied. "My head must have been up my derrière. Thank heavens I didn't toodle, or I'd have been a goner!"

Know Nothings

Did you ever notice that a lot of people who think
they know everything don't know noth'n?

No Place like Home

About nine months ago, my nineteen-year-old daughter, Rachel, wanted to get her own apartment. By doing so, she reasoned that she wouldn't have to put up with Mom and Dad interfering in her affairs.

After living alone in a one-bedroom flat for six months, she called and asked if she could move back home. Tired of working two-part time jobs and going to college, coupled with the loneliness of being by herself, she finally came to the realization that there is truly "no place like home."

When I told this story to my friend Andy (a veteran of many years in the U.S. Army), he said, "Hell, I don't blame her! As soon as I got to Vietnam, I wanted to come home!

Who Says?

My clever friend, Bob Cook, had a cartoon drawn that shows a hearse pulling a U-Haul trailer with a caption underneath that says, "Who says I can't?"

"If the idea takes off," he told me, "I'm going to start a business supplying trailer hitches to funeral homes!"

Wurstwhile

Yesterday, my son John, our friend Henry Husmann, and I went to Cincinnati to check out the Hofbrauhaus, a German restaurant that is modeled after the famous beer hall in Munich. John ordered a dinner that consisted of various kinds of German wurst (sausages).

"How's your food?" I asked.

"It's good!" John replied.

"Oh," I said, "does that mean that you've got the best of the wurst!"

No Goodbyes

This morning I took a twenty-minute drive to Decatur to have breakfast at a popular local pub, Two Brothers, with some of my friends of many years. Stopping to pick up my old eighty-eight-year-old buddy, Bob Cook, who lives in an assisted-living apartment, I knocked on his door. No answer. After repeated attempts and still no response, I was concerned and asked one of the ladies who worked there if she could open the door to his apartment. He was fine, he'd just over-slept.

"Damn, Bob," I said, "you really had me worried. I figured you had better manners than that."

"What do you mean?"

"Hell, I thought you'd checked out and didn't even say goodbye!"

One in a Million!

My son, John Schindler, has worked in the family restaurant businesses, Jimmie's Pizza and Bandido's, since he was fourteen or fifteen. He has done everything from washing dishes to managing a unit, and now he is currently Vice President of Operations. He has earned the respect of the entire management team because of his work ethic, knowledge, caring, and fairness.

Recently, I started a new company and when John walked into my office, I told him I was going to give him some stock in it. "It's going to be a real moneymaker," I said enthusiastically.

"Dad, I don't want any," he told me a little nervously.

"Why not?" I asked.

Noting the look of disbelief on my face, he said, "Dad, I don't want to disappoint you, but I didn't do anything to earn it!"

On And Off

Back again at Two Brothers Bar, as Bob Cook, Jo Jo Jauregui, and I were having breakfast, Freddy Eyanson, another old buddy, came over and joined us. "Fred, how ya do'n?" I asked.

"On and off," he replied.

"Freddy," I said, "I don't wanna know about your sex life. I just want to know how you're do'n!"

God Rules

When folks live according to their God's rules or commandments, they develop a sense of well-being, knowing that God approves their actions. This in turn enhances their self-esteem and confidence.

The Difference

The main difference between people
is the result of the way they think.

Show Off!

Just a few years ago, the newborns were kept in the nursery at the hospital, and if you wanted to see your child, you would have to go there, and peer through the large plate-glass window at all the babies until you saw the cutest one, which was undoubtedly yours.

The day after my son Jimmie made his grand entrance into the universe, I was talking to my wife, Fry, when two friends of ours, Henry and Anne Husmann, came into her room at Fort Wayne's Lutheran Hospital. After the normal exchange of pleasantries, I asked Henry if he wanted to go to the nursery to see the baby. So, while my wife and Anne chatted, Henry and I walked down the hall to view my son.

As we reached the nursery, there were two preteen girls looking through the window admiring the babies. As we were standing behind the young girls, looking over their shoulder at Jimmie, who happened to be in a bassinette in the first row, a nurse came up and started to change his diaper. When she took it off, he must have known that his daddy was in the army, because part of him was standing at attention! The girls noticed and started to giggle. Turning to my friend Henry, I said, "See, he's showing off already!" And from that day forward, his nickname has been Leroy!

A Different Look

Walking in the mall with my son, Jimmie, I said, with a chuckle in my voice, "Look at that guy! Do you see the way he's dressed?"

"Dad, if everyone were the same," Jimmie replied, "who would we laugh at?

Honor

My attorney of many years, Bob, moved to Ireland, found himself a bonny lass by the name of Pamela, and before you could say, "Liam O'Dwyer," they were married. In view of the fact that Bob was fifty-two and Pamela just over forty, they being aware that Nature's clock was quietly saying, "Not much time left, not much time," they were anxious to start a family.

At seventy years of age, since many folks attribute the things I say to my dotage and forgive me for it, I took the liberty of e-mailing Bob this advice. "Bob," I did indeed write, "if you want to start a family, you better believe in honor, get honor and stay honor!"

The Chief Reason

This past Sunday, as I was ushering at St. Peter's Catholic Church, I spotted Fort Wayne's chief of police, Rusty York, and his wife, Judy. Rusty is not only a nice guy but he has also earned the respect of the officers under him and the entire community.

After Mass, as I was handing out the weekly church bulletins to the departing congregation, when Rusty walked by I whispered in his ear, "Rusty, I'm sure glad you behaved yourself today, cause I heard the police are here!"

No Ass-Sits!

You'll never get anywhere sitting on your ass!

The Railroad Story

Years ago, someone told me a story similar to this one, by an unknown author. I liked the lesson it conveyed so much that I embellished it, and here is my version of "The Railroad Story."

More than one hundred years ago, around 1880, the railroad was king. If you wanted to travel or ship anything across the country, you had three choices: horse and wagon, riverboat, or train. Even back then, a train could go over fifty miles an hour. As a result, almost everyone who traveled or shipped merchandise any distance at all did it by rail. Needless to say, the railroad companies became very prosperous and the owners extremely wealthy.

Back then, on a hot summer day, gandy dancers (laborers on a section gang that kept the rails in good repair) were working under the blazing sun in the Arizona desert. All the work was done by hand and it was gut-wrenching, physical labor. A steel rail was thirty feet long, weighed more than three hundred pounds, and was carried and put into place by muscle, sweat, and strong backs.

Railroad ties, the timbers that held the track in place, were also very heavy. They weighed more than 230 pounds each and were soaked in creosote to protect them from the weather and to keep the bugs out. A tie not treated would last three to five years, but saturated with creosote, it would be good for twenty to twenty-five.

In addition to all of this, swinging a twelve-pound sledgehammer all day, pounding the six-inch spikes that fastened the track to the ties would not only sap your strength, it would also insure sore muscles and a good night's sleep. The backbreaking work together with the scorching Arizona sun broke many a strong man.

Now, if a train was coming while the track was being repaired, the foreman would blow a whistle and the crew on the section gang would step back and take a break until it went by. On this particular day, though, when the foreman's whistle warned the men of an approaching train, it didn't go on through, but came to a complete stop. The men had never seen a train like this. They were amazed! Not counting the engine or caboose, it had only five cars and every single one had polished brass fittings and was spotless. Among them was a Pullman (sleeping car), a dining car, and the last car before the caboose was a hand-carved mahogany car with beveled-glass windows, velvet curtains, and crystal chandeliers. Through the squeaky clean windows of that car the workers could see white-coated waiters serving several distinguished men smoking expensive-looking cigars.

Within a minute or two, its door opened and an impeccably dressed gentleman stepped out, walked over to the section gang, and asked, "Is there a Mr. Jim Johnson working here?"

The oldest man there looked at the well-groomed slicker quizzically and answered, "Yeah, I'm Jim Johnson."

"Would you come with me, please? Mr. Morgan would like to see you."

Jim followed him to the train and they disappeared into that hand-carved mahogany car.

About a half hour later the door opened; Jim and a very dignified looking man stepped out onto the rear platform, spoke for a few minutes, and shook hands. Jim then dismounted back onto the blistering Arizona sand. He rejoined his fellow workers and in complete silence and wonderment, they watched as the train started to move slowly down the track picking up speed with each chug of its steam engine, until it faded into the horizon.

Not until it was completely out of sight, did one of the men finally break the silence and say, "Who in the heck was that?"

"That was Mr. Morgan," Jim answered.

"Who's he?"

"Why, he's the president and owner of the railroad."

"Aw, come on."

"Yeah, he really is."

"Well, what did he want with you?"

"You might not believe it, but thirty years ago today, we hired in together, on this very section gang, for fifty cents a day."

Then, one of the other men sarcastically remarked, "If you were both hired in at the same time thirty years ago, how come you're still bust'n your butt fix'n these tracks and he's president of the railroad?"

"You know, I thought about that quite a lot lately, and today when I was talking to Mr. Morgan, I asked him that very question."

"What'd he say?"

"He said, 'Jim, remember when we hired in on the railroad for fifty cents a day'?

I said, 'Yes, sir.'

"He said, 'The only difference between you and me, Jim, the only difference is that you came to work for fifty cents a day and I came to work for the railroad!!!'

What are you working for? Are you working for fifty cents a day, or are you working for the railroad?

Moral: If you work for the railroad you'll go a lot farther!

Herb

During the nineteen forties and fifties, in the small Indiana town where he practiced law, Herb was the man the local gentry called upon when they had a run-in with the town's constabulary. Considered by many to be the finest attorney in the area, when he was sober, Herb would go a few weeks or months without a libation, but when he decided to partake of his favorite brewed, distilled, or fermented beverage, Katie, bar the door. There was no stopping him! Whatever he did, he did well and for several days, or weeks, he would do it so well that his consumption became legendary. When he finally decided to sober up and go back to work, he would quit drinking and not touch another drop, for weeks or months, until his next binge. Consequently, he became almost as famous for his drinking bouts as he was for his legal battles.

It was during one of these drunken sprees that he found himself quite intoxicated while driving, trying to weave his way back home. Drifting back and forth across the centerline and almost running up over the curb, he finally rear-ended a parked car, banging his head but not seriously injuring himself. In spite of his booze-soaked brain, he still had enough presence of mind to slide over into the passenger's seat.

In a few minutes the police arrived and asked him what happened. Even though he wasn't able to weave his way through traffic, he wove this imaginative yarn. "Officer, I had too much to drink, so I hired this fellow to drive me home and he rear-ended that damn car," he said, slurring his words and pointing at its smashed rear end. "Then the son of a bitch jumped out and took off!"

Thank God no arrest was made, since Herb's attorney was too drunk to defend himself.

A Painless Hurt

The only folks who call modern
dentistry painless are the dentists!

The Cigar Shops

In 1948, Christina "Tienie" Schurger, a wonderful lady in her seventies, out of the kindness of her heart, took my brother Joe and me in to live with her. I was in the eighth grade and Joe was a sophomore in high school. Back then, at least in the small Indiana towns, there was no television, so people actually would converse and tell one another stories to pass the time. As a result, Tienie told us many stories, and most of them taught us a valuable lesson. The following tale was one of them.

At the turn of the century, in the early 1900s, when smoking was very popular, a man named Phil was employed by a local church as their

74

custodian. In the two years he worked there, he was known as a good worker who did a fine job, until one day the new pastor handed him a list of chores to do. Glancing at the list with a puzzled expression, Phil looked at the pastor. "What is the matter? What don't you understand?" the pastor asked impatiently, and in an un-Christian-like tone of voice

"I can't read," Phil mumbled, quite embarrassed.

"You can't read! You can't read! Well, if you can't read, my dear fellow, how can you possibly do your job? I'm afraid that I'm going to have to let you go."

With a feeling of despair and dejection, wondering what he would do and not wanting to go home just yet to tell his wife that he had lost his job, Phil walked aimlessly, worried and desperately craving a cigarette. Looking for a cigar store, he strolled up one street and down another without any luck. After a couple of hours and still no luck, he decided he would take his meager savings and open a cigar store.

With his wife's help, he opened his first store that, over the years, grew into one of the most successful cigar store chains in the country. As a result, he became exceedingly wealthy and a pillar of the community.

The days, months, and years quickly passed, and Phil was now in his sixties, but he still stood straight and his mind was still razor-sharp. Then, one Sunday, out of the blue (only heaven knows why), Phil decided to attend services at the very church where he had once worked as a janitor.

After the service, as Phil and his wife were leaving, it was obvious to the same pastor who fired Phil that this well-groomed and well-dressed couple was wealthy. Still not recognizing Phil, but with dollar signs floating in his mind's eye, the pastor greeted them and asked Phil what he did for a living.

"Even though I still can't read or write," Phil explained, "I founded and own Phil's Cigar Shops."

"You did?" exclaimed the surprised pastor. "My God, man, just think what you'd be if you could read and write!"

"Why," Phil sarcastically answered, "I'd still be the janitor at your church!"

In conclusion, I think it's apparent that the dollars signs that floated in the Pastor's head were never miraculously transformed into the collection basket or his pocket!

The Worst of the Best

If the best team played the worst team,

and the best team played its worst and

lost to the worst team that played its best,

would the best team then be the worst?

Piled High and Deep

If someone has a PhD, MBA, MD, or whatever such letters are following behind their name they should be proud of the fact that they spent many years of study to earn that distinction. However, it is not unusual for many individuals with one or more of those titles to feel quite superior, (intellectually or otherwise), to those without them. Why, some even perceive themselves to be experts in all matters, even those that do not pertain to their field of study.

Probably the most-down-to earth PhD I ever met was my German professor, Rene D. Fabien, at John Carroll University, where I attended college between 1952 and 1956. Back then, being a farm boy from the small town of Decatur, Indiana, (population 5000), I truly didn't know what PhD stood for, so one day I asked Dr. Fabien. With a big grin on his face, he answered my innocent question with, "It means piled high and deep," which was an answer that this farm boy could really understand!

In effect, the only thing that the letters that follow one's name really mean is that the person was able to read, understand, and regurgitate the information well enough to answer their professors' questions, either orally or on a written examination. Hence, those letters in no way confer the title of Genius or Guru on anyone.

> titles of honour, learning and dignity,
>
> are not always bestowne on the wisest men.
>
> Giovanni Boccaccio,
>
> *The Decameron*

Carl

Sixty-year-old Carl had just finished getting his annual physical when his doctor, who was about the same age, asked him if he had any questions or concerns. "Doc," he answered, "I haven't had sex for several years. Since my wife went through her menopause, she doesn't want to have anything to do with it. Hell, it's been so long I don't even know if I can do it anymore!"

"Don't worry, Carl, there is nothing wrong with you. You're in good health. All you need to do is to find a gal who is willing and everything will work just fine. It did for me!"

Janice

Janice Agler is a young ninety-two-year-old great-grandmother. She is in excellent health, lives alone, still drives, and gets along very well on her own, thank you very much. But, in the past few months, even though she was always on the thin side, she started to lose weight. Worried, her daughter, Norma, took her to the doctor for a checkup. After examining her, the doctor gave her a clean bill of health.

However, Janice did explain that she didn't eat much because she didn't ever seem to be hungry. The doctor then suggested to her daughter that it might be a good idea to get her some Ensure, a nutritional meal replacement drink, to supplement her diet. When Janice heard this, she asked somewhat puzzled, "Isn't that what old people take?"

Hope Springs Up

Bertha took her eighty-three-year-old husband, Virgil, to their family doctor for a checkup. "What seems to be the problem?" the good doctor asked."

"Doctor, I'm worried about Virgil. We used to have sex every day, but lately he only wants to have it about once a week."

On hearing this, the good doctor excitedly mumbled to himself, "Yes!" realizing that, in spite of his advancing years, he also might ,be able to rise to the occasion!

The Game of Life

My son Jimmie is a senior at the University of Notre Dame and, like many college students, he parties until the wee hours of the morning, sleeps at least till noon, lives on fast food, and spends hours playing video games. During Christmas break he practically lived in the rec room in our basement, and as I walked in on him, he was playing one of his favorite games.

"Jimmie," I said, "there is more to life than eating, sleeping, and excreting. What have you done today to improve your mind or yourself?" Glancing at me, he continued to play. "In the long run," I continued, "do you know the only game that really counts? It's the game of"

"Life, Dad! The game of life."

"Well, son, then maybe you'd be better off if you started to learn how to play that game!"

Santa Comes Tonight

Coming home from our family's Christmas Eve party at our son John's home, with our younger children, Jimmie twenty-two, Heidi twenty-one, and Rachel nineteen, I asked them if they wanted to open their gifts that night or the next morning (Christmas). Jimmie and Rachel wanted to open their gifts that night, but Heidi wanted to wait until Christmas morning.

"Heidi," I asked, "why do you want to want to wait until tomorrow?"

"Because," she innocently answered, "Santa doesn't come until tonight!"

Enlightening

Wouldn't it be nice if all we had to do
to enlighten the unenlightened was flip a switch?

One Hell of a Sale

One day the Devil wanted to raise some money. His furnaces were getting old and they weren't working very well. As a result, he couldn't keep the place hot enough to insure that every single one of his wicked inhabitants stayed super toasty. So he devised a master plan to raise all the filthy lucre that he would need to buy new ones. (After all, no money was too dirty for Satan.) He would hold the world's largest garage sale. He would sell every vice and sin known to mankind, and the person who bought that vice or sin would be better at it than anyone else in the universe. He would sell lying, cheating, stealing, gossiping, lust, jealousy, and a thousand more bad things that people do.

So Lucifer and all the little devils went to work to get ready for the big sale. They collected all the vices and sins they could find, labeled them, and put them into boxes. It really didn't take too long, because there were plenty of them around. In no time at all, they were ready for a sinfully good sale.

Now Lucifer thought and thought, *How can I get the biggest crowd ever to come to my garage sale?* Suddenly a wonderful devilish idea came to him. "I know," he said with an evil grin as he rubbed his horn, pulled on this tail, and jumped excitedly up and down. "I'll tempt them!" We all know that most people can stand anything but temptation! "I'll just whisper in their ears how easy it would be to use lying, cheating, and the other vices to get what they want." So he did just that, and even he was amazed at the crowd that showed up! Why, if you weren't there, I'll bet that you know many people who were!

Soon the big sale began. There were boxes and boxes of sins and a zillion boxes of vices and they were all going fast. Before long, the crowd turned into an angry mob. People were quarreling over who could buy the deadliest sins and worst vices. Finally, even the Devil had enough of their squabbling, and bellowed, "The next person I catch fighting and causing trouble will have a hot time in my town tonight!" Now, since most people hate the night sweats, everyone behaved. This goes to show that even the evil can't stand a hell-raiser!

At last, everything was sold but one unlabeled box. One brave doomed soul asked Lucifer, "What's in that box?"

Lucifer answered, "Even though what's in this box is not a sin, or a vice, it is my greatest asset in getting people to do wrong and to give in to my temptations. It's called "Discouragement." When people are happy and content, they are extremely hard to tempt. But, when they are discouraged, when they give up hope, I've got them! I can get them to do almost anything. Then I can pull them down into the depths of hell."

When they heard Lucifer's explanation, everyone wanted to buy the box with "Discouragement" in it and they started to argue over who would get it. Finally, Lucifer held up his hand to silence the crowd and soon, the only sound heard was the roar of the hellfires. "I will only sell this box of "Discouragement" to the most evil person here," he thundered, and he called out a name and made that person come forth and swear that when that person died, it would only be given to the most evil person still living on earth.

Thus, as you go through life and sometimes wonder why some people are so hateful, deceitful, and so on, you now know how they got that way. And always remember, most of this would never have happened if people had not become discouraged!

Today the devil is very happy. He got his new furnaces while spreading sin and vice throughout the world. And rumor has it that now it's really hotter than hell down there!

Moral: Discouragement is the devil's helper!

Written especially for my grandson, Bryce Shull,
who is not averse to raising a little hell!

Lots of Bucks

My sister, Bancy, does the bookwork and makes the deposits at a nearby bank of the day's cash receipts for two of our Bandido's Mexican Restaurants. One day, she took her grand-niece (my six-year-old granddaughter), Elizabeth, to work with her. After finishing her job and making the deposits at the bank, Bancy took her home. Running in to her house, Elizabeth said, "Mom, Grandpa got so much money that he gives some to the bank!"

A Real Mother
Sometimes, Mother Nature can be a real "bitch!"

Joe Knows
Years ago, Joe and Jim got in to this huge argument over something of little consequence, which neither can remember now. Anyway, Jim got out the encyclopedia, looked up the answer, and said to Joe, "See, right here read it! I win! You owe me five bucks."

"What the hell do they know?" Joe said, with a wave of his hand, not bothering to look. "You can't believe everything you read!"

Joe never did pay the five bucks, which proves that at least Joe knows, knows how to keep his fiver!

Schindler's Second Rule of Law
Avoid Lawyers!

Flaming
Henry's Bar is not only known for its good food, it is also one of Fort Wayne's most popular gathering spots. It's a historic old place with an ornately carved back bar, wood walls, ceilings, and hand-carved

wooden booths. A cosmopolitan bar, it is frequented by artists, the theater crowd, patrons from the newspaper company next door, and many thirsty locals. Not surprisingly, since many of its guests consist of the artsy crowd, there is also a gay contingent who are regulars. In addition to all of those folks, my wife, Fry, and I have been known to frequently enjoy Henry's hospitality, libations, and fare.

This week, there was a fire in the apartment above that notable old bar. In the local newspaper was a color photograph of the building with flames shooting out of the upstairs apartment's windows, while the headline read, "Fire Heavily Damages Henry's."

The next day, Jeff, a friend of ours, called and said, "Jimmie, the headline should have read, 'Gay Bar Flaming'!

Keep the Faith

Mike, a successful realtor here in Fort Wayne, sold a house for a struggling couple who wanted to move back to Tennessee. Unbeknownst to the couple, there was a second forgivable mortgage on the house in the amount of $2,800. When the guy who had sold the couple the house was called, he knew he had the young couple over a barrel and even though he was supposed to forgive that second mortgage, he demanded the money, which he had a legal (but not moral) right to do.

The wife of the young couple started to cry because now they wouldn't have enough equity in the house to close the deal and go home. When Mike, the old softy, saw this, he said that he would forgo his $2,500 commission. The lady from the mortgage company then reached into her purse, pulled out her checkbook, and wrote a personal check for $150 so the transaction could be completed and the couple would have enough money left over to get back to Tennessee.

Not only are Mike and the lady who wrote the check first-class people who really care about their fellow man, they are also the kind of folks who renew my faith in humanity. And believe me sometimes it desperately needs to be renewed!!!

Anna

Two and a half year old Anna was the apple of her grandma "Mary Keefer's" eye, and Grandma did what grandmas do so well: she spoiled her a little, okay, a lot! As a matter of fact, Grandma referred to her as her "Precious Angel."

One afternoon, when Anna was acting up, Grandma said, "My, aren't you ornery today?"

"No," Anna replied, "I'm your "Precious Angel!"

Definition

Gambling: a fools' game!

The Wait

Not too long ago, it was considered bad manners to be late for an appointment, date, or meeting. However, today, for some reason, it seems to be in vogue. What tardiness actually says is that one is unorganized and inconsiderate. To keep someone waiting unnecessarily is truly the epitome of bad manners. So if you don't want to be perceived as rude and ill-mannered, be on time. The wait is on your shoulders!

Atonement

Why is it that when man does something wrong, or hurts his wife's delicate feelings in any way, real or imagined, she never forgets it? I honestly believe that most women subscribe to the philosophy of "I can forgive, but I won't forget!" She then proceeds to throw it in her husband's face, whenever the opportunity presents itself, thus making him pay for any wrongdoing at least a thousand times. Why, even God requires man to atone only once for his transgressions!

Finally, if someone won't forget, do they truly forgive?

Wrong Lane

Some days, life is a little bit like driving in heavy traffic.

No matter what lane you get in, it's the wrong one!

It's Everywhere!

Incompetence stalks the land!

Push'n Up

Jim, being seventy, had been having some problems with an irregular heartbeat. On a recent cold, snowy January morning, he felt pretty good, so he went out and started to shovel the drive. After about fifteen or twenty minutes, he began to feel weak, tired, and light-headed. Going back into the house, he asked his wife, Fry, to take his pulse.

"Your pulse is irregular and awfully weak," she informed him.

"Let me take your blood pressure. It's only 110 over 60. What are you trying to do, kill yourself? Don't you dare go back out there!"

After a phone call, Jim's nephew, John (JJ), came over and shoveled the drive. When he finished, he stopped in the house to say hi and, upon seeing Jim, he said, "I thought you weren't home. Why didn't you come out and help me?"

When Jim's wife explained what had happened, JJ said, "Sounds to me like you're on the edge."

"The edge of what?" Jim asked.

"The edge of push'n up daisies!"

A Great Day

I went to the hospital to see my old friend Bob Cook, who had a serious heart problem and was in the coronary care unit. "Bob," I said, "how ya' feeling?"

"Oh, I feel pretty good now, but yesterday I had a great day."

"You did?"

"Yeah, Tom Sefton, my undertaker, came up for a visit and he left without me!"

Left Out In the Cold

I recently received a very formal and impressive invitation that went as follows:

The Committee for

The Presidential Inaugural

Requests the honor of your presence

To attend and participate in the Inauguration of

George Walker Bush

As President of the United States of America

And

Richard Bruce Cheney

As Vice President of the United States of America

on Thursday, the twentieth of January

two thousand and five

in the city of Washington

It went on to say, "It [this invitation] does not constitute admission to any of the inaugural events." I guess that means that I can come, but they're not going to let me in. Bastards!

When I showed the invitation to my office manager, Holly, and Jill, her assistant, Jill said, "If you gave more money they'd let you in. It all comes down to money!"

"You're right," I answered. "Don't you know money makes the world go around? After all, aren't you working for the money?"

"No," she replied. "I'm working because you're such a nice guy."

"Then how come you keep on cashing your paychecks?"

Snow

There is nothing more beautiful than getting
up in the morning and seeing a pristine blanket
of newly fallen snow covering the countryside.
That is, until we humans go out and dirty it up!

Unlimited Potential

I believe that almost every person is born with unlimited potential. However, the negative influences and limitations imposed on us from our earliest childhood, by our family, friends, and others with whom we come in contact, chips away at that potential until we no longer "believe" that we truly have the ability to excel.

Schindler's Third Rule of Law

Keep avoiding those bastards!

No Pull

Whenever we try to motivate someone with prizes or bonuses, we must remember the story about the man in a cart who hung a carrot on a pole in front of a donkey. When the donkey tried to get the carrot, he would lurch forward and pull the cart.

However, we must realize that a carrot dangled in front of a donkey only works if he gets one once in a while. If he never gets a carrot, he'll eventually stop pulling the cart and sit on his ass.

Hard Heart

Recently seventy-year-old Jim was taken to the hospital with some serious heart problems. When his friend Joe Daniel heard about it, he phoned Jim and lectured him. "Jim," he said, "if you'd quit taking those damn Viagras and start taking your heart medicine, you'd be a lot better off.

"Wow," Jim answered, "maybe that's how I got a hard heart!"

I'm Dead?

In no time at all, Jim was lying on a cart in the emergency room with wires stuck all over his chest and a rubber electrical apparatus on his finger, all of which were hooked up to a monitor. The monitor displayed his heart rate, blood pressure, amount of oxygen in his blood, and who knows what else.

After about a half an hour, Jim glanced at the monitor. There were no squiggly lines indicating his heart rate, no blood pressure reading, or anything else, except two question marks on the screen. Worried, he pushed the nurse's call button.

"Yessss!" she answered.

"Lady, there's nothing on the monitor in here except two question marks. Either the damn thing's not working or I'm dead!"

Instead of rushing into his room screaming, "Code blue, code blue," she calmly answered, "What's wrong with it?"

I guess she figured if he could answer her question, he wasn't dead yet!

The Initial Interpretation

Charlie walked into Power's, a small hamburger shop, here in Fort Wayne, and sat down on the only available seat at the counter. Next to him were two police officers. While he was munching on his burger, he noticed that the cop next to him was wearing a bracelet with the initials **WWJD** engraved on it.

"What do those initials stand for?" Charlie asked.

'What would Jesus do,' answered the officer.

"That's not what I thought they meant," Charlie replied.

"What did you think they meant?"

"I thought they meant, '**W**e **W**ant **J**elly **D**oughnuts'!"

Not about Fish'n

When my brother-in-law, Steve Keefer, an avid fisherman, asked me to go fish'n with him, I said, "Steve, I don't really like to go fish'n."

"Why not?"

"Because I never catch anything."

"Jimmie, don't you know fish'n is not about catching fish."

"Well, what's it about? When I go fish'n, I want to catch some fish!"

"It's about getting away from everything; relaxing and enjoying the peace and quiet. No phone calls, no one bugging you. "It's great!"

"Hell, I'm so dumb," I said, "I thought fish'n was about catching fish!"

Holy

"Can you believe they gave the pope a tracheotomy?"

"No kidding, he must really be holy now!"

The Wisdom of Holden

Because of Eddie's condition, he spent a lot of time in the hospital and after one long stay he dropped by to visit his old friend Hank Freistroffer. On seeing Hank's eight-year-old son, Holden, Eddie asked him if he missed him. "How can I miss you if I never see you?" Holden replied.

Eddie's Coffin

Eddie, who is suffering from AIDS, was told by his doctor that if this new medication didn't work, there was nothing else they could do for him. Accompanied by his sister and brother, he made a trip to the funeral home to make final preparations.

Eddie picked out a very attractive casket and asked the price.

"It's twelve thousand dollars," the mortician told him.

"Can I lie in it?"

"I'm sorry, we don't allow that."

"Well, if I can't try it out, I'm going to spend my twelve grand somewhere else!"

"Okay, go ahead," said the undertaker reluctantly, afraid of losing a lucrative sale.

Eddie crawled into the casket and lay there with his hands folded and his eyes closed. Upon opening them, and seeing his brother and sister crying, he said with a sheepish grin, "It's really comfortable," and he bought it.

Later, when Eddie was telling me this story, I asked him why he had paid so much for a coffin. "Why not," he countered. "I'm going to be in it the rest of my life!"

Jimmie II's Right

My son Jimmie II said, "Dad, a meteorologist [weatherman] is the only profession I know where one gets well paid for being wrong at least half of the time.

Indeed!

No good deed goes unpunished!

Anonymous

The Castle

A man's home is his castle,

at least until he gets married!

The Mouse and the Rat

Once upon a time, there was a very hardworking little mouse. Every day she would scamper all around the barn, keeping an eye out for the nasty cat while searching for bits and pieces of food to store so she would have plenty to eat during the long winter months, which were drawing nigh.

One blustery day, shortly after the first snowfall, she desperately wanted to visit her favorite aunt, who lived in the nearby farmhouse and was very sick. "Don't worry," said the rat, whose home was in the woodpile behind the barn, "I'll watch your food for you so no one eats it while you're gone."

"Are you sure?" asked the little mouse, not really knowing if she should believe him or not.

"Trust me," answered the rat. "We rodents must stick together."

Even though the little mouse was still worried, she left the rat guarding her food and went to visit her sick aunt.

On returning home a few days later, she saw the rat lying on his back with his fat belly bulging out, taking a snooze, and all her food was gone. She was just about ready to cry when she spotted the cat out of the corner of her eye, slowly sneaking closer and closer. As fast as she could, she scurried into her mouse hole. Peeping out, she saw the cat pounce on the snoring rodent and have himself a very nice "stuffed rat" dinner.

Moral: Sooner or later lying, stealing rats usually get caught.

Dedicated to my sister Mousie, who was as nice and sweet as the little mouse!

No Boobs

Hell, I'm so old that I can remember when men were called actors and women actresses. Many actresses now call themselves actors. Is it because women now wear the trousers and men the long hair? Even if some actresses don't know the difference between an actor and an actress, there is still no way that I'm going to call them boobs!

Garage Door's Up!

Recently I was having some problems with my heart, which required a pacemaker. About a week after the surgery, Charlie, an old friend, called me up, asked how I was doing and, not waiting for my reply, continued, "You'd better be careful, I heard that when you have sex with a pacemaker, the garage door goes up!"

"In that case," I answered, "if you come over and the garage door's up don't stop!"

A Bushel?

As I was recovering from the effects of the anesthetic given to me during the surgery to install a pacemaker in my chest, Dr. Mirro came in, explained that the surgery had gone well, and gave me instructions of what I could and couldn't do. When he finished, I asked the good doctor if I could have sex. He then told me that I was a perfect candidate for Viagra since some of the medicine that I would be taking might affect my performance.

"Okay, Doc," I said, "how about sending me a bushel?"

Bennie

Shortly after Pope Benedict XVI was elected, I ran into my friend Mark Pope.

"Mark," I asked, "should I still call you the Pope, or should I call you Benedict?"

With a grin a mile wide, he answered, "Just call me Bennie!"

Artless

Sheila was celebrating her recent graduation from St. Mary's College at a party thrown by her parents. On display for all to see was her diploma, a Bachelor of Arts degree.

After reading it, her younger brother Jason naively commented, "I didn't know you had a bachelor of arts. I never saw any of your work!"

The Best & Worst

The best of the worst is still the worst of the best!

Grandpa George

In honor of his one hundredth birthday, Grandpa George was comfortably seated as his relatives, friends, and acquaintances were lined up to shake his hand and congratulate him. Finally, a middle-aged man offered Grandpa his best wishes for many more years.

"Who are you?" Grandpa asked.

"I'm John, your nephew."

"My nephew?"

"Yeah, your brother John's son."

"John? How's he doing?"

"He died last year."

"He did? How old was he?"

"He was ninety-two."

"Ninety-two? He should have taken better care of himself!"

Help'n Max

In the small town of Decatur, Indiana, in the1950s, the local police actually were there to help and serve the townspeople. If someone had a bit too much of old John Barleycorn and was pulled over, most times the officer would either drive him home or he would tell the intoxicated person, "You drive home but take it easy because I'm going to follow you all the way."

It was during these wonderful times that Max Ainsworth was parked with a girlfriend a few miles out of town, near Luden's Bridge, the local lovers' lane. Spotting Max's car, a deputy sheriff pulled up, walked over, and shined a flashlight in his window.

"Take that damn light out of my eyes," Max said, somewhat irritated at this untimely interruption.

"Hey, Max," the deputy said, "I just thought I'd stop to see if you needed any help."

"If you really want to help," Max answered, "lend me your handcuffs!"

Huh?

One evening, seventy-eight-year-old Bobby Eschoff wanted to drive over to his restaurant, Lambro's, to schmooze with his old friends and customers. His wife, Natka, concerned for his safety, told him that he shouldn't drive because it would be dark by the time he got home.

"Why?"

"Because you can't see!" she said.

"I can see!" Bobby answered.

"Besides that, you can't hear, either!"

"Huh?"

Getting There

When you know where you're going,

You usually get there.

The Good Pie

My sister Mousie knows I love rhubarb pie. Friday, as she was having lunch with my wife, Fry, she said that she had baked me a rhubarb pie.

"You did?"

"Yeah, I thought that I'd take a tiny bite to see if it was any good. It was so delicious I ate the whole damn thing!"

The Silent Message

Sometimes you don't have to say anything to say something!

Learning Problem

The problem with many students is they study

just to pass the test instead of to learn the lesson!

The English Lesson

Throughout the world, English is fast becoming almost everybody's second language. In many countries it is mandatory to take several years of English in grade and high school. In addition to that, American music, movies, and TV programs are viewed worldwide. Hence, a lot of the world's population can now speak English pretty well. I have a German friend who couldn't speak French and a Frenchman who couldn't speak German, so they conversed in English. English is fast becoming the world's second language.

Therefore, in many parts of the world, if you can't speak the local language, you generally can get along by speaking English. I think that eventually, instead of having to learn many languages, all people will have to know is two languages: their native tongue and English. Since I already know my native tongue, now all I have to do is to learn English!

No Work

Almost everyone wants a job,

but few want to work!

First Class

A first-class operation never comes in second place!

The Good Johnny

"How's your wife?" Jim asked his eighty-three-year-old friend Sim.

"She's in the hospital."

"What happened?"

"She fell. But she didn't break anything; just bruised herself up some. She's still in the hospital."

"She is?"

"Yeah, she's taking therapy."

"Is she going to have to use crutches?"

"She had crutches, but one slipped out from under her. From now on, it's a walker."

"A walker?"

"Yeah. Johnnie Walker!"

Carats Count

Craig got divorced and sometime later, Tom, an extremely wealthy businessman, married Craig's ex. One Sunday, Craig ran into Tom on the golf course and, somewhat surprised, said, "Tom, how'd you get the wife to let you play golf on Sunday? She'd never let me!"

"That's the difference between one and nine carats!" Tom answered, wearing a million-dollar smile minus the cost of the nine carats!

Definition

Gay: A happy homosexual!

The Innocents

At least 90 percent of all convicts are innocent.

If you don't believe me ask them!

Same Restaurant

Sim was born in the early 1920s, and his mother had an ample supply of breast milk. However, the lady next door couldn't produce enough to feed her newborn daughter. So like a good neighbor, Sim's mom graciously agreed to nurse her.

One day, many years later, a lady walked up to Sim and blurted out, "Your mother saved my life."

"She did?" Sim asked, somewhat puzzled.

"Yes, she nursed me when I was a baby."

"Well," Sim responded, "looks like we ate at the same restaurant!"

A Good Chance

Never miss a chance to make

somebody feel good about themselves!

The Wrath of Grapes

In the early 1930s, young Sim miraculously found himself in the middle of a neighbor's grape arbor. While he was stuffing his face with the fruit of the vine, the unhappy owner spotted him and rang up his father.

Finally, with a belly full of grapes, Sim headed home. As soon as he walked in the back door, his dad, in a stern voice, asked, "Where were you?" He no sooner got the words out of his mouth when Sim threw up what seemed like half a vineyard. More grapes than either one of them ever wanted to see.

"Well, I guess you suffered enough," his dad said with a twinkle in his eye, knowing full well that his son had learned a grapeful lesson.

Stanley "The Manly"

I asked Stanley "The Manly," my insurance agent, if he had read my book. "I didn't know you wrote a book," he said, either somewhat surprised, or thinking that I didn't have the talent. I was afraid to ask him which!

"Yes, it's called *Schindler's Tiny Tales & Whatnot*. If you get one, I'll personally autograph it for you." Taking a moment to think about it, I quickly added, "Oh hell, you probably don't want my signature unless it's on a check!"

Today's Heroes

When I grew up, in the 1940s and the early 1950s, our heroes were presidents, generals (especially from WWII), and almost anyone who was a success. We also admired the suave, well-groomed, handsome, and beautiful movie stars and singers. These were our role models that even parents wanted their children to be like.

The vast majority of today's heroes seem, at least to me, to be limited primarily to unsophisticated rappers, singers, entertainers, and sports figures that have trouble not only with their wardrobes and habits, but also with their manners, grooming, and speech.

Charlie Chaplin wore baggy, low-slung pants because it made people laugh. Why, even today, when I see someone wearing them, it still puts a smile on my face. Also, in my youth, we never saw anyone with his hat on backward or sideways, but if we did we would probably have surmised that he had just escaped from some sort of an asylum!

I can't remember even one of my heroes using foul language, being arrested for drugs, or advocating violence against women or anyone else, for that matter. In addition, they all had a reasonable command of the English language, meaning we could understand every word they spoke. These days, many of the lessons of our generation, such as, it pays to look your best, don't use profanity, be considerate of others, etc, seem to have fallen on deaf ears.

The examples set by those whom one chooses as their heroes will have a profound impact upon his or her life. If one has decent, honest, and compassionate role models and heroes, it will affect them in a positive, successful way, because that's how they'll endeavor to be. However, if one emulates those who have self-destructive, negative qualities, sooner or later they will acquire some of those same qualities, because that's what they obviously admire and want to be like. Consequently, their lives will suffer because of it.

Of course I'm aware that almost every generation has been concerned that their youth was going to pot, but this is the first generation I know of that, instead of cooking in, or sitting on one, they smoked it! Would it be logical to conclude that the reason for their outrageous dress and behavior is that the pot has gone to their heads?

Body Talk
You'd be surprised what your body will tell you,
if you'd just listen to it!

Ponce I've found it!
The "Fountain of Youth" is in your thoughts.

Where to Go
When Dr. Barbish finished his examination of Jim, he said, "I want you to get a CAT scan of your stomach and pelvic area."

"Where do I get that done?" Jim asked.

"My nurse will be in, in a minute, and tell you where to go."

"Doc, I know you probably won't believe this, but someone is always trying to tell me where to go!"

Good Advice
To lottery buffs: Don't spend it until you win it!

They Can't Help It!

Not too many years ago, if someone drank too much, he was called a drunk and was scorned by his friends and neighbors. Sooner or later, a relative, an acquaintance, or someone would pull him aside and say something like, "What the hell is the matter with you? Where's your backbone? You've got a wife and family and a good job. If you don't straighten up and quit drinking, you're going to lose everything! Look what you're putting your family through! It's high time you get your crap together and start acting like a man"!

Today, if someone drinks too much, he's called an alcoholic. But he can't help it, poor guy, he's addicted! He has a disease! (Probably got it at down at the Boom Boom Saloon!) Why, I even read where they are now considering designating obesity a disease! I wonder if they'll call it "the Fat Disease!" If so, they'd better warn folks to stay away from the "Chocolate Factory" so they don't catch it! Also, they should tell them that if they don't want to catch two diseases at once, they'd better steer clear of "Drunk'n Doughnuts"!

If alcoholism and other excessive or addictive behaviors like smoking, gambling, overeating, etc., are diseases, they are the only diseases I know of that you give to yourself and can cure yourself of any time you truly make up your mind to do so! Wouldn't it be nice if we could cure cancer, heart disease, and other real diseases like that?

Furthermore, isn't it in the best interest of the psychiatrists, psychologists, social workers, and medical profession, to have these behaviors designated as diseases? After all, doesn't a disease have to be treated by a professional (at reasonably exorbitant fees, of course)?

What they, the shrinks and the medical community, are really doing when they designate ordinary human weaknesses a disease is taking away the personal responsibility for one's actions. After all, how can an alcoholic, a gambler, or any of the others take responsibility for his or her actions when they have a disease that caused it? This is precisely the rationale that the drunk, excuse me, I mean the alcoholic, uses to justify his actions when he says to himself, "Man I caught this disease and since it ain't my fault and there's nothing I can do about it, I might as well go down to the Boom Boom Saloon and enjoy it!

Fast Gas!

George recently graduated from Franklin College and, as a reward for all his hard work, and because he didn't like to take long walks, he bought himself an SUV. Now, you don't have to be a PhD to know that SUVs have a well-deserved reputation for being gas guzzlers.

Last week, when he came up to our cottage to visit our son Jimmie, I said, "George, take me for a ride in your SUV. I want to see which moves the fastest: your gas gauge or your speedometer!"

Everyone thought my joke was a gas except George. He has to buy it!

Little strokes fell great oaks.

Ben Franklin

It Doesn't Pay

Those who spend more than they make,

will sooner or later go broke.

So be prudent in your financial affairs,

because fiscal irresponsibility doesn't pay!

The Good Ones

In the 1950s, Dr. Peck, a well-know Decatur, Indiana, veterinarian and quite a colorful character, was approached by a couple of slick-looking salesmen in Two Brothers Bar. When they tried to convince the good doctor to invest $5,000 in an oil well, he told them, while trying to suppress his mirth, "Why I couldn't do that. It would take all my ones!"

The Skivvie on Sim's Fondest Memory

During breakfast this morning with my eighty-three-year-old friend, Sim Hain, at the West End Restaurant, I asked him what his fondest memory was of growing up in Decatur, Indiana. Without any hesitation, he said, "It was when I met my wife, Pat. I was a junior in high school and she was a sophomore. We've been married sixty-one years. Why, just this past week, we put on some old records and danced in our Skivvies!"

Mindless

If an empty room seems larger than one that is furnished,

why does an empty mind seem smaller?

Ass Sits

If you act like an ass, sooner or later,

someone's going to sit on you. After all,

doesn't everyone like to sit on their ass?

Clayson's Concern

During the Great Depression in the early 1930s, Clayson's son's dream was to become a doctor. One day, his dad took him to Loyola University, in Chicago, which was about a six-hour trip from their hometown. When they were finally ushered into the admission officer's impressive office, Clayson, with hat in hand and moisture in his eyes, said, "I'm just a poor man, but my son John," as he turned to look at him, "wants to be a doctor."

As a result of that visit, arrangements were made for his son to attend Loyola University. When his education was completed, Dr. John Carroll returned to his hometown, Decatur, Indiana, and for many years not only practiced medicine there, but was the town's only surgeon. Needless to say, in no time at all, he became one of the most respected and loved residents of that small community, and all because of Clayson's concern.

Definition

Bureaucrat: a non elected public official who has

absolutely no common sense and couldn't care less!

Quoting Bob

The more you help people the weaker they become.

Bob Sweigert

Half-Fast

This past weekend I had a slight stroke, and as my concerned son Jimmie was rushing me to the hospital, I said, "Slow down, son; another minute or two won't make any difference. Besides, I'd rather take twice as long to get there than go twice as fast and only get halfway there!"

Hold the Party!

After arriving at the hospital, I was checked over in the emergency room and was admitted. As soon as I was comfortably situated in my bed, I picked up the phone and called my son John, who is the Director of Operations for our small restaurant chain, Bandido's. "John," I said, "hold the party, I ain't go'n nowhere!"

The Good Care

The day before my stroke, I'd had an appointment with my cardiologist and after a thorough examination he had told me that I was doing great and there were no restrictions on my activities. So as I lay in the hospital the morning after my stroke, when my cardiologist walked into the room I said, "Doc, thanks for taking such good care of me!"

A Shining Star

Always do your best and you'll stand out from the crowd
like a bright shining star. For there are a billion stars in the sky,
but when we look at the heavens, we only notice the brightest ones!

You Don't Say

Too many times, what people say is not necessarily true or accurate!
Anytime you are told, hear, or read anything, you should
temper it with your own experience, common sense, and
good judgment. For if it goes against the grain of any
one of these, it probably isn't accurate or true.

The Red Bracelet

At the hospital, one of the questions that the nurses always ask is, "Are you allergic to anything?" If so, they put a red wristband on your arm that lists your allergies.

When my brother and sister-in-law, Steve and Mary Keefer, heard that I was in the hospital, they paid me a visit. After chatting awhile, Steve noticed my red wristband and asked, "What does the red bracelet say? 'Do not resuscitate'?"

He Didn't See a Thing

After Steve and Mary left, I was taken downstairs for a CAT scan to see if there was any damage to my brain. The following morning, when the doctor came into my room, I asked him what the CAT scan showed. "I couldn't see a thing," he answered. That really worried me, because now I didn't know if he meant he couldn't see any damage or he couldn't see a brain and I was too afraid to ask!

It's Hard to Beat the Band!

A Nice Choice

When it comes to choosing your life's mate,
a nice girl is always a better choice than a beautiful bitch!

Better Go!

When Mother Nature calls, better go!

A Timeless Thought

My seventy-one years have taught me that the old Latin saying *tempus fugit* (time flies) is definitely true. If everyone truly understood how accurate this phrase really is, perhaps they'd make better use of their time and as a result live a more meaningful and productive life.

for there is no greater errour in this life, then the losse of time, because it cannot bee recovered againe

Giovanni Boccaccio
The Decameron

There will be sleeping enough in the grave!

Ben Franklin

Nothing!

Do you know what happens when a wife gets mad at her spouse?

Nothing!

An Old Bastard

Today at St. Peter's, during our conversation, Pat Lombardo said that she was at least twelve years older than I am. When I told her my age, seventy-one, Madeline, her daughter, who was also standing there, said with a shocked look on her face, "I thought you were about fifty-five."

"Thank you," I replied. "Many people think I'm a bastard they really don't know I'm an old bastard!

A Helping Hand

The only helping hand you
can really count on is your own!

Don't Tell It!

"Honey," a wife might say to her husband, "I want you to tell me the truth. How do I look?" Or, she might ask, "Does this dress make me look fat?" To these and other such leading questions, a shrewd man recognizes that the wife really doesn't want to hear the truth and, for reasons of self-preservation, flattery is a much wiser course to take. For, to tell the truth is to listen to the tongue toll endlessly!

Moral: When the wife says that she wants to hear the truth about her looks or appearance, don't tell it!

The Unteachable Sense

You can't teach common sense!

The Incredible Shrinking Man

Why is it when I get out of the water, after a dip,

I feel like I'm only half the man I was before?

Driving Disabilities

Have you ever noticed that many people

with handicapped license plates drive like they are?

Lying Hurts

I had a friend who was an exceptionally strict father who punished his children severely if they misbehaved. As a result, they were deathly afraid of him and if he questioned them about any wrongdoing, they would lie or do anything necessary to keep from feeling his wrath. Consequently, they soon learned from experience that lying would keep them from being spanked or punished. And so, to this very day, they still lie instead of telling the truth.

Quite frankly, I took the exact opposite approach. I told our kids that no matter what you do, if you tell me the truth, I won't give you a spanking. But if you lie to me, you're definitely going to get it. So as our children grew up, they told the truth, because they learned that the truth wouldn't hurt them, but lying and deceit would.

Commonsense Rules for Raising Great Kids

Never call your child a derogatory name like dumb, stupid, fat, ugly, worthless, etc. For each time a child is called such a name, a piece of his/her self-worth is torn from his/her very soul, which slowly but surely destroys their self-confidence. ("After all, if my parents think I'm stupid, I must be!") Before you make a negative or cutting remark, remember the old saying "If you can't say something nice, don't say anything at all," and your children will be the better for it!

Never show favoritism, for it makes the other children feel less worthy and loved.

Always encourage your children to do their best in whatever endeavor they undertake. When children know their parents support and believe in them, it builds their confidence and motivates them to excel,

Praise your child for each accomplishment, no matter how small, for it will aid in developing a healthy self-image and an "I can do it" attitude.

Give your children unconditional love, for every child needs his/her parent's love more than anything else! A parent's love is an amazing elixir that makes children feel happy, content, and secure. What's more, they will return that love a hundredfold and pass it on to their children.

The Bogeyman
If most golfers put as much time and effort
into improving their circumstance as they do their handicap,
they would never again have to worry about the financial bogeyman!

Avoid the Familiar

You'd have a lot fewer friends if you had to live with them!

Or, as the old adage goes, "Familiarity breeds contempt."

A Humane Lesson

Most dogs are smart enough

not to bite the hand that feeds them.

Don't you wish the human animal was too?

How'd You Do That?

While working the host station at our Portland, Indiana, Bandido's restaurant, a lone man came in and I asked, "One for dinner?"

"Two," he replied. "My wife's parking the car. She'll be in in a minute."

"Would you mind telling me something?"

"No, what?" he answered.

"How'd you train her to do that?"

Jay's Genes

Today when I was going over the color that I wanted the wall under a wainscoting, painted in one of our Bandido restaurants, my sister Fran said, "Are you really going to paint that red?"

"Sure," I answered.

"I don't think that's going to look right. It doesn't match the rest of the wall"

"Don't worry," I assured her. "It'll look great."

"Ask Jay," (our gay assistant manager who was sitting nearby) she said, looking for support. "He doesn't like it, either."

"I think it clashes," he agreed.

Being somewhat annoyed, I said, "Jay, what qualifies you as an expert on interior decorating?"

Not missing a beat, Jay replied, "My gay genes!"

After laughing heartedly, you might say I was happy but not gay!

Hail to the Chief!

Today, at Sunday Mass, I sat behind Fort Wayne's police chief, Rusty York, and his wife, Judy. During the Mass, after the priest says, "Peace be with you," the congregation answers, "And also with you." The priest then says, "Let us offer each other the sign of peace."

After that, the parishioners shake hands with those nearby and say something like 'Peace" or "Peace be with you." When Rusty turned around to offer me a sign of peace, I said, "Rusty, I don't know if I should say 'Peace be with you,' or 'Hail to the Chief!'

First Timers First!

At St. Charles Catholic Church, as the proud parents and grandparents were anxiously awaiting the First Holy Communion Mass to begin, the teacher in charge made the following announcement over the intercom: "Would all the children who are making their First Communion for the first time please go to the back of the church."

The Tongue Is Mightier Than the Gun

When Vice President Cheney accidentally shot his friend while hunting, the liberal media and late-night comedians were relentless in portraying him as a bumbling buffoon. However, this unfortunate incident is miniscule in comparison to the damage done by even one biased comedian or commentator, for they can destroy more men with their tongue than a thousand men with a gun! And it's no accident!

His Job Bugs Him

At Bandido's, a small but wonderful Mexican restaurant chain, they employ a pest-control service to insure that their stores stay bug free. A short while ago, Kim, the general manager, saw a dead bug on the floor and put it in a plastic container to show the pest-control man on his regular monthly visit. When he showed up, she told him that she wanted him to take a look at the bug she had found. "I don't want to see it," he replied "I hate bugs!"

Hair Today

My wife, Fry, and I were making our funeral arrangements and she was rattling on about something. I don't know what it was because, like many husbands, when it comes to their wives, I also practice selective hearing. Anyhow, during her soliloquy, I happened to glance in a mirror that was hanging on the wall. Finally, finishing her monologue, Fry said, "Oh well, here today, gone tomorrow."

"No," I replied, noticing the glare on my dome. "Hair today, gone tomorrow!

Ethel?

As my wife and I were watching the national news, the announcer explained that as an EMS ambulance was rushing a lady about to have a baby to the hospital, they got caught in a traffic jam. Noticing that the time had come, they quickly pulled into a gas station, where the EMS technicians delivered a healthy girl. Looking over at my wife, I said, "I wonder if they'll call her Ethel?"

What Counts

My sister-in-law, Mary Keefer, is the principal at Bishop Luers Catholic High School, here in Fort Wayne. From time to time, to increase its enrollment, she gives recruitment talks at Sunday Masses in the local Catholic churches. At one such Mass, as I sat in my pew and listened to her explain the benefits of a Catholic education, she said something that I'll never forget: "At Bishop Luers, we not only teach our students how to count, we teach them what counts!"

Toochie Loochie

Mary was babysitting for her four-year-old granddaughter Anna, when she told her not to pick her bottom. "But, Grandma," Anna replied, "doesn't your underpants ever get caught in your toochie loochie?"

110 Percent

If 100 percent of something is everything, how can anyone give 110 percent? Or am I confusing myself with the facts?

Three Hail Mary's

As Bishop D'Arcy was speeding along, trying to make a meeting on time, he was pulled over by an officer of the Indiana Highway Patrol. As the officer approached the bishop's car, the good cleric unbuttoned his coat so the officer could see his priestly garments. Assuming someone up there was watching over him, he then said, "Hello, Officer. I'm Bishop D'Arcy."

Unimpressed, the police officer replied, "I'm Officer Smith. Now, may I see your driver's license and registration, please?"

Back at his squad car, the officer checked the holy man's documents and license plate number. Returning to the bishop's vehicle, the officer, who must have been a Protestant, gave him back his papers along with a speeding ticket for his worldly wrongdoing.

A few days later, after the good bishop told this story to a group at a fund-raiser, he fondly recalled when he was a young priest administering to the faithful in Boston. "Back then," he went on, "when a good Irish cop would pull me over, he would just say, "Faaather, better watch your speed and say three Hail Mary's!"

He SAT On His Ass-ets

Today, many colleges and universities place greater emphasis on SAT scores than performance. A student who does very well on his SAT exam but has mediocre grades simply because he didn't apply himself will be welcomed with open arms, while the student with a lower SAT score but who worked his tail off to get good grades is denied admission. This leads me to the conclusion that only in the surreal college world would anyone value potential more than performance. Even an idiot would choose the person with a proven track record over one who just SAT on his ass-ets, for there is nothing more pathetic than unused talent!

Definition

Eve: the first "Adam smasher."

My Best Shot

When people tell me that our daughter Heidi
looks just like her mother, I reply, "You know what really
upsets me? I gave it my best shot and she looks like her mother!"

The Mighty Mind

I was raised in an orphan's home, where everyone had to do his share, and then spent seven years living and working on a farm, doing a myriad of chores like milking cows, slopping the hogs, feeding the chickens, baling hay, and shoveling manure (actually we had another word for it), which was all hard, physical work. As a result, I believe the old adage, attributed to the Amish, at least in this area, that goes "the harder I work, the luckier I get" should be changed. For if one can think of an easier, better, more efficient way, he will accomplish much more, with half the effort, than the man who uses just his muscles and might. Therefore, I think it makes more sense to say, "The smarter I work, the luckier I get," for "the mind is mightier that the muscle."

It's a Good Thing

Bob, like many fathers, was explaining to his six-year-old daughter how tough he'd had it when he was a kid. When he finally finished, she said, "Gee, Dad, it's a good thing you came to live with us!"

The Luckiest Man

A wealthy man was being interviewed aboard his luxurious yacht, live on TV. After a tour of the vessel, the reporter, who was obviously overwhelmed by its grandeur, blurted out to the owner, "You must be the luckiest man alive."

"No," replied the owner. "My best friend is! He can enjoy all this and it doesn't cost him a penny."

From Myself

I gave two tickets to a private suite in the Conseco Arena to my friend Max Luking, an Indianapolis Pacers fan. A few days later, when I ran in to him, I asked him how he had enjoyed the game. "It was fantastic," he answered. "We had box seats, a great view, and there was plenty of free food and drinks. Why, it even included a complimentary private parking spot. You kind of feel like it separates you from the riffraff."

"Then it's a good thing I didn't go," I said.

"Why?"

"Because it would've separated me from myself!"

Little Thinking

Men who think with their little

Heads seldom get prenuptial agreements!

Moral: The little head is not stuffed with brains.

"You cannot help men permanently by doing for them

what they should do for themselves."

Abe Lincoln

First Prize

My wife, Fry, and I were enjoying the Monday night meatloaf special at Henry's, one of our favorite restaurants, when we heard a lady, who was seated at the bar just a few feet away from our booth, repeatedly using the f-word and swearing like a college kid in a frat house. Looking over, I espied not a lady, but an unkempt, straggly-haired, big-mouth broad. As she continued her profane tirade, I told my wife, "If I were her husband, I wouldn't take her to a dog show! You know why?"

Shaking her head, Fry answered, "No, why?"

"Because she'd probably win first place!"

Donovan's Get'n Old

While having a beer with my old friend Jack Donovan, who has known my family for years, I happened to mention that my sister Mousie just turned eighty.

"Eighty," Jack repeated, "God, I'm get'n old!"

Sometimes

Sometimes the right thing to do

is not always the best thing to do.

Nobody but Us

When Jack's wife informed him that he had to clean out his bedroom closet, he asked, "Why?"

"Because we're going to redecorate the bedroom."

"What for?" he sincerely questioned. "We're the only ones who ever see it!"

Mini Is Mighty

I usually buy a minivan and, recently, when a friend asked why I didn't get an SUV, I answered, "Because a minivan cost a lot less, has more room, rides better, uses less gas, and the insurance is cheaper. So why would I buy a SUV?

However, I must admit that the SUV is more of a status symbol, if that is your priority. But at least, in my opinion, the decision to buy one is based solely on ego, not common sense.

Moral: Whenever ego battles common sense, ego wins by a knockout!

That's Smart

He was so smart…he couldn't

tell a flutist from a flautist!

My SUV

Look at me in my SUV,

All puffed up with vanity.

Driving it was a blast,

Till I filled it with gas.

Now all my money's at BP!

Now that's Mean!

One of my favorite sayings was coined by a famous comedian. I think it was either Rodney Dangerfield or Henny Youngman, and it goes something like this: "When I drink my wife gets mean!"

A Foxy Dog!

When I lived in Decatur, Indiana, back in the seventies, my dog Domino was free to roam the entire town, including the surrounding area. Sometimes he'd be gone for days, but he always came home, tired and hungry. Evidently, like anyone who travels a lot, he learned some valuable lessons. The following story is one example.

On one of my many jogging trips to Hanna Nuttman Park, as usual I took my dog Domino along. After we finished our run and were walking through the park, Domino spotted a lady and her young son, about ten years old, having a picnic. I wasn't concerned as he headed over to the boy, who was enjoying a piece of the Colonel's chicken, because Domino was a very friendly dog. As he got within ten or fifteen yards of the boy, he raised one of his front legs and limped right up to the kid, who was by now feeling sorry for him. As the boy reached out to pet him with his empty hand, Domino grabbed the chicken out of his other hand and took off like a bat out of hell on all fours!

Light Up

The bishop and Father Bob were having a conversation when Father Bob pulled out a pack of Marlboros and, while searching through his jacket's pockets for a light, the bishop commented, "That's not good for your health. When are you going to quit?"

"When you let me have sex," Father Bob answered with a smile.

Not missing a beat, the bishop snapped back, "Go ahead light up!"

Benedict

Father Jeff was instructing the seventh grade-class when they heard that the new pope had chosen the name of Benedict XVI. Immediately on hearing the news, Emily started crying.

"What are you crying about?" asked the good priest.

"I don't like him already!" sobbed Emily.

"Why not?"

"Because, why would anyone name himself after Benedict Arnold?"

Not Much

You can always tell a woman, but you can't tell her much!

Everyone Can Pass!

My brother-in-law, Hank Freistroffer, once told me something that I believe is true, when he said, "Even the dumbest kid in the class will pass if he does his homework."

Useless Gifts

When many people buy someone a gift, they buy what they want them to have instead of what the person really wants or needs! Since one shouldn't look a gift horse in the mouth, most folks graciously accept the gifts, but never use'em, making them useless and wasteful.

The Great Acting Game

After viewing a few World Cup soccer matches, it became apparent that, quite often, after any contact with a member of the opposing team, no matter how insignificant, many players would fall to the turf and wither in pain until an official called a foul and gave their opponent a yellow or red card. Then they would jump up and continue playing more vigorously than before, because in addition to having a penalty called in their favor, they also enjoyed a short rest.

This tactic seemed to be obvious to everyone in the stadium except the referees. Quite frankly, I think that at the end of every soccer game, an award ceremony should be held and an Oscar presented for the best acting performance. In addition, the "Boot" should be given to the player deemed guiltiest of overacting!

Fair Game

Why is it that in today's world, almost everyone, at one time or another, claims that he/she was, or still is, discriminated against except the "white male"? Is it because he has never been discriminated against, or is it because, in our "politically correct" society, he's the only creature left who is fair game?

A Bad Day

When my wife, Fry, came home, she noticed the red light flashing, two messages on the answering machine. Turning it on, she heard the following:

"Fry, this is John [her brother]. We have one square left on the board for the Indianapolis 500. I know you'd like to play, so out of the kindness of my heart, I'm going to put you on the board. You can pay me the five dollars later. Have a nice day."

The second message went as follows: "Fry, this is John again. We just finished drawing names for the race, and you drew Sam Hornish, Jr.; he has the pole position and is the favorite. Everyone is ticked off because, out of the kindness of my heart, I put you on the board and you got the best draw. Have a bad day!" Click!

However, both Sam and Fry had a great day. Sam won the race, and Fry won a hundred bucks! But, poor John, let's just say he had a bad day!

The Real Man

Observe a man's actions; scrutinize his motives; take note of the things that give him pleasure. How, then, can he hide from you what he really is?

The Analects of Confucius

Sweat'n

One noon, at our cottage on Lake Wawasee, my son Jimmie and I decided to drive the boat over to the Frog, a tavern with docking facilities, for lunch. Not because the food is memorable, but because we wanted to relax and spend some time together.

When the waitress delivered our Diet Cokes, she said, "Oh, you don't have any napkins" (to set the Cokes on to soak up the condensation). "I hate it when they sweat all over!"

"So do I," Jimmie agreed. "That's why I don't date fat girls!"

Hell on Earth

Even if one doesn't believe in God or eternal damnation, I think that almost everyone will agree that whoever lies, steals, kills, does drugs, or violates one or more of society's laws, sooner or later, will suffer the consequences. Such people not only run the risk of ruining their good name and possibly their health, but they could also be fined, jailed, or perhaps even executed, depending on the offense. In other words, if people do bad things, bad things will happen to them and, as a result, they make their own hell right here on Earth. In addition, if they are really bad, they could quite possibly wind up having one hell of a time in Hades!

Write It Down!

As folks grow older, they seem to have a tendency to be more forgetful, and I think it's safe to say that most of the elderly believe that this is a natural part of the aging process. This might be partially true, but quite frankly I honestly feel that there are also other reasons for their forgetfulness. Of course, ill health and stress can have an impact on one's memory. In addition, is the fact that there are so many things to remember in a busy person's life, even a much younger person would have difficulty remembering them all.

When I was a young man, I wrote in my Day-Timer what I needed to accomplish each day, so I wouldn't forget anything. Obviously, such a mental lapse at that time would have had absolutely nothing to do with either my age or my memory. However, over the years, I learned that if I truly wanted to remember something, all I had to do was really concentrate on remembering it and I would. This taught me that "Concentration is the mother of memory!" Still, to play it safe, I would write it down, because it is a foolproof method of keeping me from forgetting daily tasks and appointments.

No matter how sharp or brilliant one's mind is, nobody can remember everything. So let me paraphrase an old adage for you, and hopefully you'll get the point! "Even the dullest pencil is sharper than the keenest memory." So damn it, write it down!

They Are

It's not what people say that defines them,

it's what they do that tells what they're really made of!

Or, as the old saying goes, "Actions speak louder than words!"

Above Average

A while back, I read something to the effect that the average person flatulates (passes gas) eleven to thirteen times a day. Hot damn, I always knew I was above average!

Relatives, Friends & Acquaintances

Relatives, friends, and acquaintances are a lot like old shoes.

Some are a nice fit with a lot of soul, and some just plain stink!

The Bread Man

It always amazes me when I hear folks, generally women, raving about how much money they saved by buying this or that on sale. Excuse me, but when people spend their money, how in the world do they do figure they saved it? Does it really matter if they bought the items on sale or paid full price? Isn't the result the same? Meaning, now they have less money than they had to begin with.

If I had a hundred dollars and saved some more money, wouldn't I now have more than a hundred? Conversely, if I spend some of that money, no matter how good the deal, wouldn't I now have less? Logic would tell any rational person that spending money is not exactly the same as saving it. Hence, a sale is just a means for merchants to sell the gullible a bill of goods, while lightening their purses and convincing them that they actually saved money. If only I could get my wife to understand this, I'd save so much dough they'd call me the bread man!

Before, During, or After?

As I was having breakfast with my old Decatur friends, Bob Cook, who will turn ninety this month, Sim Haines, who is eighty-five, and Joe Jauregui, who is only seventy-three, Sim mentioned that tonight, a really good movie, *Broken Trail*, was going to be on TV. "It's four hours long," he went on, looking at Bob. "So you'd better take a nap."

"Before, during, or after?" Bob quipped with a twinkle in his eye and a shit-eat'n grin on his face.

When Fashion Is In, It's Out!

Whatever catches the fancy of the Hollywood elite, the TV celebs, and the movers and shakers' tastes in clothing, restaurants, style, etc., will always be fashionable until it becomes so fashionable, it becomes unfashionable!

There was once a very trendy restaurant in New York City, not too many years ago, that was continually packed with celebrities. Over a period of time, the local populace found out about it and also started to frequent that establishment. When this happened, the socially elite (at least as they perceived themselves to be), moved on to another trendy spot, but the locals continued to pack the place. About this time, Yogi Berra was asked if he still frequented that particular restaurant and his answer went something like this: "That place is so popular, no one goes there anymore [meaning, of course, none of "the "in crowd"]!"

Fashion is also based on how difficult something is to attain. The fewer people who have the means to acquire it, the more fashionable it will probably become. For example: A century or two ago, the whole of Europe was pretty much an agrarian society, which meant that most people's lives were spent in the countryside working on farms and in the fields. As a result, any part of their bodies that was exposed to the sun and elements was deeply tanned and weathered. Only the ruling class, clergy, the wealthy, and those who didn't have work in the fields had soft, fair skin. Hence, since only a few could maintain their natural flesh tones, light skin became fashionable and highly desired. In the novels from those times, truly attractive and desirable women almost always had "skin as white as milk."

In the United States, which is truly a melting pot of people of every race and color, intermarriage between the races, given enough time, will darken the features of the general populace. When this happens, instead of people wanting a nice tan, it will undoubtedly be fashionable to have skin as white as milk because it will not be as common, and thus will become all the rage. So again, what is now fashionable will once again be unfashionable.

Before the discovery of oil in their dry, desolate deserts, the Middle Eastern countries were quite poor and the vast majority of their populace barely had enough food to survive. As a result, most of the people were quite thin. Only the aristocrats and the wealthy had a surplus of food, which enabled their women to maintain fuller figures. Since these women were the exception, they were considered more attractive and desirable to the Arab men. Even to this day, many men in those countries still prefer their women a little more substantial. However, given that their economies have vastly improved (thanks to the world's demand for oil), it is almost certain the general populace will pack on the pounds since there is now plenty of good food available, and therefore it will be much more difficult to stay thin. Then, what is now fashionable (the fuller figure) will, in no time at all, become unfashionable and thin will definitely be in.

Also, what seems to be fashionable today with a lot of the younger generation (I'm referring to the lack of good manners: profanity: hats worn backward or sideways: baggy, low slung pants that exposes their hopefully spotless underwear seems to be so popular that perhaps, with a little luck, these trends also will soon have run their course, and good manners, proper English, and sensible attire will again become fashionable. We can only hope! After all, anyone can be a slob!

True Contentment

Unless you like the person
you see in the mirror, you will
never attain inner peace and contentment!

Mad

Never make a decision when you're angry,

because later on, it just might drive you mad!

Horse Around

He who horses around generally doesn't go too far!

The Vertical Man

Charlie ran into his friend, seventy-five-year-old Carl, at the coffee shop and asked how he was doing.

"I'm just glad to be vertical," he answered, "and to think I spent a good part of my life trying to get horizontal, but now I'm just happy I'm vertical!"

Olde Harry
(an Olde English term meaning "the Devil")

rats, weevils, and lawyers were created by Old Harry.

George Eliot

The Mill on the Floss

Wives Rule!

If it's true that in the Bible it says,"Wives should be subordinate to their husbands in everything," then why is it generally the other way around?

They Never Forget!

Talking to my office manager Holly Tapp, I wisely, at least in my opinion commented, "Women never forget anything, and they won't let us [men] forget they don't forget!

"Yeah," Holly said and smiled, "And don't you forget it!"

You Can't

You can't improve anyone; they have to improve themselves!

And unless they have an intense desire to do so they won't!

A Whim

Never buy anything that you don't really need, on a whim especially when on vacation. For it will usually sit on a shelf collecting dust until you put in a garage sale, or give it away.

Thank God!

Today, my friend Tom Locke made me realize how fortunate we all are when he said, "Thank God we don't get all the government we pay for!

The Long Walk

In the 1950s, as young Tom Hurst was cruising around town with his buddy Freddy, he ran a red light. Within a few seconds, the sound of a wailing siren and the flashing red lights in his rearview mirror told Tom that he'd better pull over.

On approaching his car, the officer asked Tom why he'd ran that red light. Tom, his courage bolstered by old John Barleycorn, told the officer in no uncertain terms that his eyesight must be failing, because he didn't run no red light. Freddy, who sat there listening, his wit dimmed by the same cheap booze, butted in with, "You ran that light, might as well admit it!"

"Damn you, Fred," Tom responded, angry at his friend's betrayal. "Get out of the car. I ain't taking you home. You're gonna walk!"

"Tom, give me the keys," the officer ordered, holding out his hand. "You're not drive'n anywhere, you're coming with me."

In spite of his precarious situation, that very night Tom got his revenge. For as he rode in style to the police station, Freddy had plenty of time to mull over his betrayal and to sober up, on the long walk home.

Young Joe

Back in the 1960s, Joe Trentadue, a hardworking businessman from Decatur, Indiana, asked me during a conversation about Social Security and other government programs for the elderly, if I knew who was supposed to take of him when he grew old. "In other words," he went on, "who's supposed to take care of Old Joe?

"Who?" I asked, not knowing what to say.

"Young Joe!"

Boring!

A dish without a little spice is boring!

Oh to B

Today, I called my sister Margie to wish her a happy birthday. After some small talk, I asked, "Are you eighty-three?"

"No," she replied. "I'm eighty-four. How old are you now?"

"I'm seventy-two."

"Oh to be seventy-two again!" she lamented.

Wiser is better!

He was a wise man who invented beer.

Plato

But he was a wiser man who drank it!

Schindler

Tony Meets Carla

In the 1960s, a twenty-year-old brunette (I only mentioned her hair color because I didn't want you to think she was blond!), Carla, worked in the record shop at L.S. Ayres, a department store here in Fort Wayne, Indiana. One day a young man rushed into the shop and hurriedly said, 'Tony Bennett, San Francisco.'

Carla, naively believing he was introducing himself, replied as she extended her hand, "Carla Walker, Stryker, Ohio."

Prepare Thyself

You can accomplish anything you desire,

if you prepare yourself.

The Indelible Marks

Since these days it seems like half of the adult population has one or more tattoos, I assume that it's the "in" thing. In a previous essay, I explained that most fads are popular until they become too popular, and then they go from "in" to "out." However, when tattoos finally go out of vogue, as all fashionable trends sooner or later do, they'll still be "in," that is, in the skin! So be careful of the indelible markings you put on your body and where, because your current friend may not be the tattooed one, and he/she will not be thrilled about your ex's name permanently inscribed on your unexposed body parts. No ifs, ands, or butts!

More BS

In 1956, I graduated from John Carroll University, with a BSS degree. In case you're wondering what BSS stands for, it simply means more BS than just plain BS.

The Unspoken Truth

One should always be able to speak the truth. However, now a days a lot of folks are reluctant to do so if the truth is not considered politically correct. Suppressing the truth in favor of political correctness has been instrumental in spawning many despotic, socialistic, and fascist societies. And we all know what happened to them! Finally, what is ofttimes considered "politically correct," is not always "correct"!

Needless

Sometimes when we've had all we need,
we still haven't had all we want!

Nobody's Perfect

Even smart people do stupid things!

Wearing Down

If we understand that, given enough time, the wind will wear down a rock, then it should be no surprise that the hot air generated from a woman's mouth by its continuous running and nagging will eventually wear down the even the most reluctant spouse.

Brian

Brian, a friend of mine who happens to be gay, works a lot of long hours and, as a result, many evenings he doesn't get home until nine or ten o'clock. One such night, when he again came home late, his significant other, Josh, sarcastically remarked, "Who are you? I don't know you."

"Sounds just like a wife," I commented. "Are gay partners as catty?"

Nodding his head, Brian emphatically answered, "Worse!"

"Worse," I mimicked. "In that case, I'm really glad I'm straight!"

"You can't buy class!"

Jerry Henry

Rock's Commandments

- Keep holy the Lord's Day, unless you're more than fifty miles from home!

- Thou shalt not steal, unless it's from the government!

- Thou shalt not covet thy neighbor's wife, unless she's really hot!

Foolish Spending

We've all observed that, for the most part, politicians spend the taxpayer's hard-earned money with reckless abandonment. But I seriously doubt they'd spend their personal funds in the same irresponsible manner. This brings me to the conclusion that "It's always easier to spend someone else's money foolishly!"

The Rating Game

Three of the main factors in rating a university are: how many PhDs are on its staff, how many are published, and what is the magnitude of their research. However, by its very definition, a university is an institution of higher learning, comprised of a faculty and a student body. And, I think it's safe to assume that the faculty is there to teach the students. Therefore, if the primary purpose of a university is to educate, shouldn't how well they accomplish that task be the most important consideration in evaluating it?

On most college campuses there is a Web site where the students rate their professors and, if they have a low rating and a lousy reputation, students avoid them like the plague. Quite frankly, students could care less about what kind of a degree their professors have, if they're published or not, or if they have a great reputation for research. Their only concern is, can they teach and are they going to learn anything in their class?

Hence, it seems to me that the logical thing for the president of a university, his or her staff, and department heads to do would be to go to the students Web site and get the true lowdown on the good, the mediocre, and the horrible. Then, armed with that information, they could make the changes necessary to insure the student body receives the quality education they deserve. However, it is extremely unlikely that this approach will ever be taken, since common sense does not run amuck in academia.

The Sober Hangover

During a conversation with my office manager, Holly Tapp, I mentioned that, "I must really be gaining weight. This morning when I tried to put on a pair of pants that I wore last winter, I couldn't get them buttoned up."

"You don't look like you've gained any weight," she replied, either being polite, or sucking up.

Grabbing the roll around my belly, I said, "Look, I'm hung over and I haven't even been drinking!"

Questioning

If you ask a lot of questions and listen carefully to
the answers, you'll be surprised how much you'll learn!

Mc & Mac

I emailed me old chum, Roberto O'Connolly, of Dublin, Ireland, and asked if it is true that Mc and Mac originally meant 'son of,' and he answered thusly:

"Once again, you are completely right. Mc or Mac does mean son of so, MacBitch well, you get the idea. Typically, you would find more Mac among the Scottish and Mc among the Irish, but of course there are crossovers."

Then he asked this perplexing riddle, "So how do you identify a Scotsman by looking under his kilt? If he has a quarter-pounder, he's a MacDonald!

The Rooster and the Goose

Early one morning, just as the rising sun began to peek over the horizon bringing the day's first light, a proud rooster perched himself on the top rail of the barnyard fence, stood as tall and straight as he could, and noisily greeted the coming morn with his cock-a-doodle-doodling.

His loud crowing awoke the goose out of a deep slumber, and as a result he was really honked off. Waddling over to the rooster, he nastily asked him why he was making such a racket when all the other animals were trying to sleep.

"It's my job," said the rooster. "Every morning my master expects me to awaken him when the sun comes up and as long as I do, he will take care of me."

"Well, he feeds and takes care of me and I don't have to do a thing!" said the goose as he waddled back to his nest, feeling quite superior because he didn't have to work.

Each day, the rooster not only had to awaken his master, he also had to watch over the hens while the lazy goose did nothing but eat and eat and sleep. One day, when the goose was nice and plump, the farmer came, took that fattened bird, and had a very nice dinner for his family and himself.

Moral: If you don't have something to crow about, your goose is cooked!

Written especially for my granddaughter, Kelli,

who is beautiful, smart and, more importantly, nice.

So, as anyone can see, she really has something to crow about!

Stuff

My old friend (he's not really *that* old!) Fritz once told me, "The problem with owning assets is that they have to be managed," which obviously takes time, effort and, too often, money. The same holds true for all of your personal items (stuff). They also have to be taken care of (managed). That's why I hate stuff. Stuff not only creates clutter, it costs money, it has to be cleaned, dusted, stored, and otherwise cared for. Furthermore, isn't it obvious that the less clutter we have in our lives, the more peaceful and serene our lives will be?

Kama Sutra

In December of 2000, Anil Doshi, my Indian friend, and I took a trip to India, where he was born and raised, to visit his family and see some sights. One of the interesting places we visited was the Chittaurgarh Fort, erected in A.D. 500. Built high above the nearby city, it encompasses more than 700 acres. During the Middle Ages, approximately 65,000 inhabitants lived within its walls. Today, about 5,000 people still reside there. Once inside, it doesn't seem like a fortress, probably because its sheer size and mountainous topography make it difficult to see any of the defensive walls that surround the fort.

The most impressive structure within the fort is the Victory Tower. It stands about a hundred feet high and has very ornate carvings on the entire exterior. Obviously, it was built to celebrate some sort of victory.

On boarding the bus, as we were about to leave the fort, a man and wife were missing from our group. Despite an extensive search of the fort, they were nowhere to be found. In about a half hour or so, our guide finally returned and asked if anyone knew where they were. "I know where," I replied. "They're on top of the Victory Tower, committing Kama Sutra!" None of our fellow passengers thought it was as funny as Anil and I did. Maybe it was because they'd never committed it!

Definition

Eccentric: Anyone who
thinks or acts differently from us!

The Taj Mahal

The highlight of our Indian trip was the city of Agra, where the internationally renowned Taj Mahal is located. Built by the Shah Jahan as a mausoleum for his favorite wife, Mumtaz-i-Mahal, in the 1600s, it took 20,000 workers twenty-one years to construct that magnificent edifice. It is the most expensive tomb in the world, and is as beautiful as the pictures that you have seen of it. Made of Indian marble, which supposedly is the hardest and finest marble anywhere, it was interesting to learn that the decorations on its exterior are not painted on but are actually semiprecious stones inlaid in the marble.

Inside, there are two monuments that look like tombs, encircled by a carved alabaster railing. This, in turn, is surrounded by a chain-link fence to keep the tourists from jumping over the alabaster screen and desecrating the tombs. However, the bodies of Shah Jahan and Mahal are not actually buried in those tombs. They are buried directly below, since Muslims must be buried in the ground (earth).

It is also against the Muslim religion to have graven images (pictures and statues); consequently, the inside of the Taj, aside from the tombs and alabaster screen, is rather plain. Also within, there are no electric lights, only natural light, so it's rather dim.

Another interesting tidbit is that the Shah was going to build himself an identical tomb nearby, only in black marble. His son thought it would be too costly and would bankrupt the treasury, so he seized the throne and threw his father into prison, where he remained until his death a few years later.

Our guide then explained that a lady on a previous tour told him, "The Taj Mahal is definitely the world's greatest erection to a woman!"

Between

When a lady asked Arthur for directions, he said, "You have to speak up, I have hearing aids and I'm a little hard of hearing."

Raising her voice, the lady explained, "I have a friend who has hearing aids, but she can only wear one at a time because when she wears them both, they make a squealing sound. Do yours do that?"

"No," Arthur replied "But maybe it's because I have something between them!"

The Smoker's Number

Whenever I see someone smoking, I wonder what he/she is thinking. Nowadays, the adverse effects that smoking has on one's health has to be known by anybody with a brain. Therefore, it is extremely difficult for me to understand why anyone would want to light up.

Regarding the young kids who start smoking, it's almost certainly due to peer pressure or just wanting to look cool. In addition, the fact that many of their parents probably smoke, thus setting "the example," doesn't help matters much. Still, anyone who smokes is either clueless, i.e., living in la-la land, or they believe that the other guy is the one who is going to get lung cancer, emphysema, or suffer from the plethora of the other health problems that smoking causes.

If smokers are asked why they don't quit, they'll give you an answer like, "I enjoy it," or "If I quit, I'll gain weight," or "I can't, I'm addicted." All of these are nothing but smokescreens for the true reasons, which is they lack the willpower, or they simply don't really want to quit, or they refuse to face the facts about the dangers of smoking.

For years I tried to get my sister to quit, and she claimed she couldn't. But when she started spitting up blood and her doctor told her she had lung cancer, she stopped immediately and never smoked again, which verifies, at least in my mind, that anyone who really wants to quit can. She was extremely lucky because after they removed a half of one of her lungs, she is now cancer free. But not everyone will be that fortunate. The risk one takes by smoking is a little bit like spinning a roulette wheel. Sooner or later, given enough time, the smoker's number will definitely come up and when it does, he/she had better pray it's not up permanently!

Three Ways

Walking with our son Jimmie in Foster Park, here in Fort Wayne, we were discussing estate planning, when the subject of death came up. "If I had a choice," I tried to explain to him, "there is one of three different ways that I'd like to go."

"I don't even want to hear the first one!" Jimmie quickly interrupted, unable to contain his mirth.

Understand?

If you don't understand it, don't sign it, buy it, or do it!

Not Teachers

"Dad, you wouldn't believe the number of professors who can't teach," my son Jimmie told me as we strolled through the campus of a prestigious Midwestern university, from whence he recently graduated. "Hell the reason they call them professors," he went on, "and not teachers, is because half of them can't teach!"

Family, Friends, and Florida

Maybe I'm cut from a different piece of cloth, but when I was asked if I was going to move to Florida when I retired, I answered, "Why would I do that?" My family, children, grandchildren, and all the friends I've made over my entire lifetime live here in Fort Wayne, Decatur, or nearby. Besides, there's nothing down there that I want. Also, it's too damn hot in the summer, there's too much traffic, and it's too damn crowded, especially during the tourist season.

Furthermore, a lot of folks who retire and move to Florida move back after a few years simply because they miss their family and old friends. Finally, it is always better and less painful to learn life's lessons from observing the actions of others rather than go through the same experience yourself. Consequently, not being as dumb as I look, there is a lesson or two to be learned here. First, since my family is the most important thing in the world to me, why would I move well over a thousand miles away from them? And secondly, there are no friends like old friends.

It Prevents What?

How many times have you watched a game when the team that's winning suddenly goes into a prevent defense or a stall and, as a result, loses the game? What that team is actually doing is trying not to lose instead of trying to win. It's hard for me to understand why they don't continue doing what was working and got them ahead in the first place. In my opinion, the only thing a prevent defense or a stall does is prevent a team from winning!

Valueless!

For the first twelve years, our public school system is compliments of the taxpayers. Since it is free, too many parents and, as result, also their children, do not place much value on that education. For example, if parents were paying their hard-earned dollars to send their children to a parochial or private school and their children came home with bad grades, I guarantee they would get what-for. After all, aren't they paying good money to see their kids get a first-class education? So they'd better damn well apply themselves. This is, without a doubt, one of the major reasons parochial and other private schools, almost without exception, turn out better educated students.

To further illustrate this premise, over the years I bought each of my kids a car, which most of them trashed. But later, when they had to buy their own vehicles, they all, without exception, took much better care of them. Why? Because, since they'd spent their own hard-earned money, the car now had value. These lessons validate that anything that is free has very little or no value!

Obviously

To many, the obvious is not so obvious!

A Hell of a Trip!

It was so long ago that I don't remember who it was, but someone asked me if I knew the definition of a salesman. I thought it was so clever that I'm going to tell you. "A Salesman is someone who can tell you to go to hell and make you look forward to the trip."

Thanksgiving Gobblers

Are folks who eat too much turkey on Thanksgiving gobblers?

The Prodigal Heir

Some time ago my brother Joe told me this story. As he was watching the news one evening, a man who had inherited a small fortune was being interviewed.

"You mean to tell me," the interviewer asked, "that you inherited over three million dollars five years ago and now you're broke! My God, man, what did you spend it on?"

"Well," answered the prodigal heir, "I spent about two and a half million on wine, women, and song, the rest I spent foolishly!

Moderation

It has been well known for countless generations that "moderation in all things" is the key to a happy, healthy, and long life. Perhaps one of the reasons why there are so many miserable people is because they simply ignore these words of wisdom.

Boredom Is the Father of Fatigue

Lunette

In 2000, Donna Brooke and her mother, Irene Freistroffer, went to Rome, Italy, for the Roman Catholic Jubilee celebration. On the ride up the escalator to the Sistine Chapel, Donna was standing next to Friar Thom Lombardi, the tour guide, reading a brochure describing Michelangelo's celebrated ceiling.

The descriptions repeated "Lunette with Job," "Lunette with Daniel," and so forth. A little confused, Donna turned to the good Friar and asked him who Lunette was, since she sure seemed to get around. As soon as the priestly guide could contain his mirth, he explained that a "lunette" was one of the semicircular, lunar-shaped, painted panels in the Sistine Chapel's ceiling.

It might also be noted, since everyone in the tour group was so tickled by Donna's "Lunette," that, in this case at least, ignorance was heavenly bliss!

The Cute Masseur

At the beauty shop, as Jill was getting her hair done, the masseur from the massage parlor next door walked in. "He sure was cute," Jill commented, with a big smile on her face, as she told Holly and me all about him the next morning. "I'd sure like to get a massage from him," she went on, "but he probably charges fifty dollars."

"What does he rub for fifty dollars?" I, not so innocently, asked.

"That's what we'd like to find out," Holly said, with a big smile on her face.

"Well, I just hope he doesn't rub you gals the wrong way!"

Togetherness

Sometimes too much togetherness is too much!

Make'n Room

At the supper table, my three-year-old grandson, Joe Steigmeyer, asked his mom, Jenny, if he could have some cookies.

"Joe, you'll first have to eat some of your food," Mommy said. "There's no room, [meaning on his plate] for dessert."

Using both hands Joe pushed his plate and everything in front of him toward the center of the table, looked at his mom, and said; "Now there's room!"

Hard Advice

The hardest advice to follow…is one's own!

Frank Didn't

In the 1960s, Don installed a new set of quality shower doors for Frank Sinatra. On completion, he handed Frank the bill. Glancing at it, Sinatra questioned, "Four hundred dollars for shower doors?"

"Wanna buy them at Sears?" Don countered.

Frank didn't, he paid!

Shamus and the Saint

My wife, Fry, has a beautiful flower garden and right in its midst is a statue of Saint Francis. As our son Jimmie stood there admiring the flowers, Shamus, the family dog, ran into the garden, lifted his leg, and peed on all over the statue. *Boy*, Jimmie thought, *I guess the animals really do like him!*

I Just Luv'em

As I lay on the gurney, waiting to be wheeled into the operating room for foot surgery by Dr. DeTommaso, an Italian American and one of the premier podiatrists in the Fort Wayne area, he asked if I had any questions.

"No," I replied, "but I want you to remember one thing,"

"What's that?" he asked.

"I just want you to know I like Italians!"

Quaaludes

As I was having a beer with an old friend, he told me how he used to do drugs when he was a young man. "Quaaludes, that was the best stuff," he reminisced, with a big smile on his face. "That's how I burned myself, got these scars (as he displayed them for my inspection), and split my head open. Hell, if they still made them, I'd probably be dead."

"Yeah, Steve," I replied, "it really sounds like the best stuff, especially if you're into self-mutilation and a short life!"

The Vacuum

On Christmas, after my daughter Rachel explained that Dan, her boyfriend, had given her a badly needed vacuum cleaner, I said, "Wow, he must really be sucking up!"

An Obvious Truth!

Big mouth little brain!

All Aboard!

Today, my wife, Fry, went to breakfast with several of her lady friends, where they were to exchange Christmas gifts not to exceed five dollars each in value. This evening, when I came home, she showed me a new broom that Jamie King gave her at that gathering.

"She gave everyone a broom," my wife explained.

Not being one to resist a good opening, I asked, "Did she give you gals a broom to clean up with, or was it for transportation?"

Youth

Youth is a wonderful time to grow up in!

The True Test

Yesterday, my wife and I went mattress shopping. After testing several different models, we finally went back to the one we thought was the most comfortable. As we lay there, trying to decide if it was truly the best choice, Susan, the salesclerk, was extolling its wonderful features. When she finally paused, I said, "Why don't you throw a blanket over us and we'll give it the real test!"

Holly's Folly

As I was composing a business letter with the help of Holly, our office manager, I said, "Sometimes when I'm writing, I leave a letter or word out because my mind works faster than my hand."

"That happens to me when I'm talking," Holly interjected. "Sometime I'll leave out a word because my mind works faster than my mouth."

Sorry, ladies, but I just couldn't control my chauvinistic tongue when I said, "And that's unusual for a woman!"

Keep Trying!

"my odds for success dramatically improve with each attempt."

John Nash, in the film *A Beautiful Mind.*

Logic

Logic is not logical…to the illogic!

More Good Advice from Fritz

Fritz, my old friend, convinced me to have a legal agreement drawn up on a deal that I was about to go into, when he gave me this advice: "Certainty ends confusion!"

The Mouse and the Cowboy

Recently Mouse, an attractive lady, was telling me about the fling that she once had with a cowboy. "He was so gooood looking!" she said. "And not bad in bed, either!" It was obvious by the gleam in her eye and smile on her face that she enjoyed reminiscing about the time she'd spent with him.

"Mousie," I said, "I just want to know one thing about the cowboy."

"What?"

"When he was in the mood, did he take his spurs off?"

The Crazy Good-bye

After I was told the following story by Sim Hain, a previously mentioned friend, I asked him if it was true. "Who cares?" he replied, "It's a good story!" So here goes.

Louis "Satchmo" Armstrong, the great musician and trumpet player, once had an audience with the pope and when they were done and Satchmo was about to leave, the pope made the sign of the cross with his right hand, blessing him.

After that visit, one of his friends asked him what impressed him the most about the pope.

"Well," Satchmo answered, "he had on this tall, pointed hat, a big fancy robe, this huge ring, and red shoes. But what I dug the most was his crazy good-bye!"

Get'n Old!

You know you're get'n old if, the
"highlight of your day" is reading Dr. Gott's column!

The Good Life

If partying and the good life are so good,
why are we usually better off without them?

God-Speak

During the Communion ceremony at Mass, a cell phone rang. Pulling it from her purse, a lady, oblivious to good manners and class, answered the call and began talking in a loud voice as she walked toward the altar. When she finally stood in front of the priest to receive Holy Communion, he angrily looked at her and said, "Lady, you'd better be talking to God!"

A Healthy Lesson

Why do the people who take the least medications
seem to be the healthiest?

What Else?

Three joys in Jimmie's life are Notre Dame, watching college football, and fishing. After dating Kate for a few years, I asked him if he thought they would ever get married

"Dad," he answered, "I think she'd be a good wife. She's a great cook, keeps her apartment spotless, loves Notre Dame, likes to watch football and loves to fish."

"Gee, son," I replied, "what else could any man ask for?"

She Remembers

Bob, on turning ninety-two, asked one of his lady friends, "Do I look ninety?"

"No," she answered. "But I can remember when you did!"

Thanks a Lot!

Marion didn't have a way to get to work, so for several weeks JoJo, a coworker, gave him a ride. On the last day they rode together, when Joe picked Marion up, he gave JoJo a bunch of green onions. That evening, as JoJo was dropping him off at home, he asked, "Are you gonna give me any gas money?"

"But I give you them thar onions," Marion protested. "That's all I got." And the last thing JoJo heard, before the car door slammed, was: "But if thanks will pay ya, thanks a lot!"

Up the Hill

"Big Al" Bowen was a lot taller and more muscular than his old buddy Gene Hill. Consequently, Big Al would frequently tease Gene about his short stature and his having to look up to him. One day they ran into each other at a party and Gene introduced Al to his two sons, who were even taller and huskier than Big Al.

"Wow," Big Al, said to Gene "Those sure are some big boys!"

"Yeah," Gene answered. "Now how do you like looking up the Hill?"

The Last Time

"The last time I got out of jail, I didn't know
if I should go straight, or become a politician!"

Lary

The Best Man

A week ago last Wednesday, my son Jimmie, asked his sweetheart, Katie, to marry him. The following Monday, he asked me to be his best man. Surprised, and truly touched, I answered, "I thought you were supposed to ask your best friend."

"Dad, you are my best friend!"

Choked up and holding back the tears, I replied, "Son, I'd be honored to be your best man."

Experience

When some folks say they have twenty years of experience, what they actually have is one year's experience twenty times, since they were either lazy, didn't care, or were too stupid to learn anything after the first year. I think, to most folks, it's fairly obvious that an idiot with twenty year's experience is still an idiot!

Moral: Experience is vastly overrated by the inexperienced!

The Truth

When Lary came in late for work, his boss, somewhat peeved, asked him why he was late. "Because I was laid out drunk," he answered.

"Gee," the boss replied, somewhat taken aback, "I've never heard that one before."

I guess he just wasn't used to hearing the truth.

Fanaticism

Since fanaticism is based on misguided faith, hatred, and emotion and has nothing to do with logic or common sense, it is practically impossible to reason with fanatics or change their outlook or beliefs.

Hang on, Kenny!

When Kenny saw Terry, his dentist and friend, at his eightieth birthday party, he complained about having a toothache. "Whenever you get a chance," Terry informed him, "give me a call and I'll fix you right up."

"I can't take Novocain," Kenny reminded him.

"That's okay," Terry replied. "I'll give you some gas."

"I can't take that, either. It makes me sick."

"In that case, I'll give you some Viagra."

"Viagra," Kenny said with a worried look on his face. "What for?"

"Because without a painkiller, you're going to need something to hang on to!"

Easier

After discussing with my contractor, Brad Kees, the installation of a large decorative palm tree outside our restaurant, I asked if it was necessary to contact the local authorities for approval. "I don't think so," he replied. "After all, it's easier to ask for forgiveness than it is to beg for permission."

Nice vs. Nasty

It's hard for me to understand why some people are so nasty or just plain downright mean. Maybe it's because they don't truly understand that if one is honest, fair, and considerate in his or her dealings, then others will treat them in the same manner. In addition, they will also have earned the respect, loyalty, and goodwill of everyone. And once this is earned, people will do almost anything to help or assist them.

Conversely, if one is rude or nasty, he or she will be treated in kind, and will, most assuredly, not earn anyone's cooperation or respect. As a matter of fact, people whom they mistreat will do almost everything in their power to discredit or destroy them. Consequently, in the course of human relations, nice is always better than nasty.

The Spiteful Spouse

Over the years, Marianne thought her husband's friend, Harry, was one of the nicest guys she had ever met. He was soft-spoken, polite, and very considerate. Marianne never met his wife, but she assumed that she must also be an awfully nice person.

Then, one day, in his golden years, Harry died. At the showing, Marianne met this little old lady, who was Harry's wife. After extending her sympathy, Marianne sincerely went on and on about what a nice guy Harry was. Finally, the little old lady, with a look of disgust on her face, blurted out, "You didn't have to live with the son of a bitch!"

Marianne was so shocked that she damn near fell into the coffin. Thank god she caught herself, because as much as she liked Harry, she didn't like him that much!

I'll Let You Go!

When you're talking on the phone and the other party says, "I'll let you go now," what they really mean is, they're bored or they have to go, or both!

One Hell of a Homily

Last Sunday our pastor, Father Widmann, gave a sermon on "hell." After Mass, as he was standing in the back of the church greeting the departing parishioners, I said, "Father that was one "hell of a homily!" He gave me a "devilish" smile, which made me believe that he'd really enjoyed giving his flock a little bit of hell!

The Treadmill

Trying to keep his boyish figure, Jim Carroll was warming up on the treadmill at the local YMCA when his friend, Jimmie, spotted him. After the usual exchange of pleasantries, Jimmie said, you know those who walk on treadmills don't go very far. And even if they go twice as fast, they still don't go any farther!"

The St. Patrick's Boogie-Woogie

Seventy-two-year-old Bob recently retired from playing the organ at St. Peter's church. Today, I asked him if sometimes when he practiced and no one was in church if he ever wanted to play the boogie-woogie.

His eyes lit up and he answered, "Sure. But this [St. Peter's] organ is pretty old. It's a lot easier to play it on St. Patrick's organ. It was built in the 1920s and has a lot more features." Which brings me to this conclusion: you're never too old to boogie-woogie, unless your organ is!

Say Cheese!

Whenever someone takes your picture,

why do they insist that you grin like an idiot?

Sometimes, aren't you just tempted to say, "I don't want

to grin like a Chessy Cat and I don't feel like saying cheese!"

Definition

practical joke: giving pain while assuming the aspect of mere fun

Edgar Allan Poe

The Good Folks

Tonight, my wife and I drove to Berne, a small Indiana town of about three thousand, to pay our respects to the family of an old friend of mine, Earl Habegger, who recently passed away.

On the edge of town we stopped at the first gas station to inquire where the funeral home was. As I was about to walk into the station, a gentleman, about sixty, was coming out.

"Sir," I addressed him, "I wonder if you could tell me how to get to the Yager-Kirchhofer Funeral Home?"

Looking at me, he replied, "Where Earl Habegger is?"

"Uh-huh."

"I'm just leaving, so why don't you follow me? It's just a few blocks from here. I'll take you around the back. That's where the parking lot is."

Following him, I said to my wife, "Isn't that nice how he went out of his way to help us?" You can sure tell the difference between big-city and small-town folks!"

Afterward, I got to thinking, *Wouldn't it be great if everyone treated each other like they lived in a small town?*

Signing My Life Away

This morning I had an appointment to have an MRI. I soon as I walked in, the receptionist gave me some forms to fill out and sign. The last one was a consent form for an intravascular contrast injection. On that form it stated, "in rare cases, it [the injection] can cause permanent disability and death."

After reading it, I asked the receptionist, "You mean you want me to sign for a procedure that could kill me?

As far as I know," she informed me, "it only affected one guy, and they took him away."

"What happened to him?"

"I don't know. I never saw him again!"

You'll never believe this but, I signed immediately!

Al's Going Nowhere

After finishing breakfast, at Two Brothers Tavern, Big Al Bowen, Don Christianer, and Jim Price sat awhile kibitzing. Finally, Big Al said, "I gotta go."

"Where ya going?" Don asked.

"Nowhere."

"Nowhere?"

"Yeah."

"Well, when you get there, let us know!"

Not Yet!

Too many old folks just sit there

and act like they're on their last leg.

As a matter of fact, the only difference between

them and the dearly departed is, they're not buried yet!

The Lost Troopers

As they were about to enter a restaurant, Indiana State Troopers Kevin Kubsch and Andy Barker were met by a motley looking guy with a long beard, who looked like he had just escaped from ZZ Top.

"You guys lost?" he asked the troopers.

"No, why?"

"Cause this ain't the doughnut shop!"

The Magnanimous Banker

After receiving an overdue notice, Arthur contacted the bank and explained that he not only had made the payment, but the check had already cleared his account. The loan officer then explained that he would look into the matter and get back with him.

A few hours later he called back as promised. "I'm sorry," the banker said. "We did receive your payment, but mistakenly applied it to another account. But now, we've got it all straightened out. However, I want to assure you that this in no way will affect your credit or standing with the bank."

"You know," Arthur sarcastically responded, "that's really nice of you. Thanks for not punishing me for your mistake!"

The Wisdom of Confucius

"The Master used to say that he owed his accomplishments to the fact that he was not employed by the state."

The Analects of Confucius

The "Benefactor"

Contrary to what they believe, what made this country, the United States of America, the greatest nation mankind has ever known was not the politicians, the bureaucrats, or the attorneys, it was the free enterprise system (capitalism). Capitalism is based on the idea of giving people the freedom to make their own economic decisions and to enjoy the fruits of those decisions, or suffer the consequences. It also provides the incentives that grease the wheels of business and industry. As a result, the free enterprise system has produced the highest standard of living in the history of mankind.

I know this will probably surprise those above-mentioned egotistical know-it-alls, but the free enterprise system, first and foremost, is responsible for creating the business and industry that provides the goods, services, and jobs, which makes everything else possible. For without business and industry, there would be no jobs; hence, there would be no one to pay the taxes that every government needs to survive. And, without taxes, there could be no infrastructure (roads, sewers, public education, police, etc.) that is a must for every progressive and orderly society.

In addition, if there were no jobs, there would be no means for the masses to acquire the funds necessary to purchase the basic necessities of life. Sooner or later, this would result in chaos, anarchy, and possibly even revolution. Therefore, any government, politician, or leftist that does anything to harm their "Benefactor" (business and industry) is in effect hurting not only the economy and the country, but, worse yet, they are hurting the working man and woman. Understanding this, I believe every rational person should thank God for our capitalistic, free enterprise system and do everything in his or her power to ensure its success and survival.

Unfortunately, there are segments of our society who cannot seem to comprehend this fundamental truth. If only they would look through clear eyes that are unencumbered by preconceived notions, and beliefs; then perhaps they could also see the commonsense practicality of the free enterprise system and how it benefits everyone.

No Secret

It's no secret that too damn many people have their hand out. They want everything free, as long as someone else is paying for it. They want free medical care, free education, free housing (at the very least, government subsidized), free food (food stamps, etc.), plus who knows what else.

First, it would be interesting to know how many people there are on the dole who really don't qualify. If I were a betting man, I'd bet plenty. For those who are, much of the blame belongs to the bureaucrats who administer those programs and have no regrets or second thoughts about their reckless disregard of squandering the taxpayers' money.

Secondly, do you think that those who are on government assistance realize that nothing is free, that all the benefits they get cost the taxpayers dearly? Thirdly, do you think they give a damn?

It doesn't take a college degree from John Carroll University to understand that all those government handouts are compliments of the taxpayers. Therefore it should be plain to all those who really don't belong on the dole and the bureaucrats who make it possible that they are not only ripping off Uncle Sam, they are also screwing the hardworking taxpayers, which includes their friends and neighbors. Bastards!

The Golf Club

Not too long ago, several investors approached Jerry Henry, a very successful Indiana businessman, and asked if he would be interested in investing in a Country Club. "It's a sweet deal," they explained. "We can buy it for less than appraised value!"

"I don't like country clubs," Jerry responded.

"But it includes a free lifetime membership and a thousand dollars of free golf a year."

"I don't play golf and I don't want to belong to no country club. I don't like them!"

After some more futile discussion, the investors retired to an adjoining room and in a few minutes returned. "Tell you what Jerry. We'll give you five hundred dollars worth of free golf a year and five hundred dollars worth of free food. And you can let your family and friends use it. How's that?"

"That sounds okay, but I don't like country clubs."

"What if we change the name from a country club to a golf club?"

After a brief pause to mull it over, Jerry, nodding his head and with a million-dollar grin, replied, "Okay, that sounds a lot better, count me in."

Stressed to Death

I think it's fairly reasonable to assume that more people have died from worry and stress, than have ever died from overwork. At least I don't know of anyone who worked themselves to death. Do you?

Gentle Does It!

Sitting in a dental chair while my dentist, Mark Friedrich, was preparing for an extraction, I said, "Doc, I want you to remember what I tell my wife before we go to bed."

"What's that?"

I say, "Honey, you're going to be gentle now, aren't you?"

They're Killing the Goose!

The education required to be a doctor is very demanding and requires hours and hours of difficult and demanding study, over a period of many years, before he/she can go into practice. As a result, I don't think any rational person would begrudge a doctor for making a comfortable living. Thank God there are some wonderful doctors whose primary concern is for their patients' well-being. However, in too many cases, care for the "almighty dollar" has taken precedence over care for the patient.

Doctor's offices are often set up like an assembly line. First, you sign in at the front desk and give your financial and insurance information, to make sure they're going to get paid. Then, after a generally lengthy wait, you are ushered into a small room, where the nurse questions you and gets all your health information ready for the doctor while he's going from room to room visiting other patients. Finally, he comes into your room, spends a few minutes, and is on to the next patient.

Obviously, this system is designed so doctors can visit as many patients as possible per day. Time is money, and the more patients they see, the more money they'll make! The emphasis seems to be on making money rather than caring for the patient. A routine visit of a few minutes, to any doctor, may cost hundreds of dollars and, if anything is serious, thousands. In addition, if surgery is required, you're talking thousands, if not tens of thousands.

Recently, I had a procedure where I was stuck with a needle, several times in my back, to ascertain where my pain was coming from. I was in the room where the procedure was performed for all of twenty minutes, during which the doctor (pain specialist) stuck me ten times. His bill was eight thousand dollars, or eight hundred dollars per stick. Not too bad for a twenty-minute job! And this is just the tip of the iceberg. I'm sure many of you have been stuck with a much larger bill.

Not too many years ago, almost all hospitals were nonprofit institutions, with some sort of a religious affiliation. Many were run by nuns. Then, a hospital's primary function was to mend and heal both physically and spiritually, not to make huge profits. If they just broke even, they were elated.

Today, I think it's safe to say that the majority of hospitals are for profit institutions. Of course, the more money they make, the happier Wall Street and the stockholders will be. As a result, just a few days in a hospital may cost more than the average person makes in a year.

It is also my belief that the reason so many hospitals spend money like an idiot who just won the lottery is to keep their earnings from being too exorbitant, which would cause them to, sooner or later, come under government scrutiny for sticking it to the general public.

Overall, the medical industry has turned into a money machine, in which doctors, hospitals, pharmaceutical companies, medical suppliers, et al, are making untold fortunes off the backs of the unfortunate folks who desperately need their help!

Finally, there is so much money and so much greed involved, that if it continues, the government, by necessity, will someday step in and socialize our entire medical system. And we all know what happens when the government runs anything! If or when this happens, the entire medical industry will not only have let their greed destroy one of the world's best health care systems, they will also be guilty of killing "the goose that laid the golden egg," *a*nd they will have no one to blame, but themselves!

Right On

No matter where you go to church, or what your religion is,

if it helps you to be a better person, it's the right one!

Liquor and Longevity

The horse and mule live thirty years

And nothing know of wines and beers.

The goat and sheep at twenty die

And never taste of Scotch or Rye.

The cow drinks water by the ton

And at eighteen is mostly done.

The dog at fifteen cashes in

Without the aid of rum and gin.

The cat in milk and water soaks,

Then, in twelve short years…it croaks.

The modest, sober, bone-dry hen

Lays eggs for nogs, then dies at ten.

All animals are strictly dry

They sinless live and swiftly die.

But sinful, ginful, rum-soaked men,

Survive for three score years and ten.

And some of them, a very few,

Stay pickled till they're ninety-two!

Author unknown

Never Grow Old!

Refuse to grow up and
you'll never grow old!

The Round Table

If you've ever wondered why, when several people who see the same thing, are asked to explain what they saw, each person's description will be somewhat different?

Just imagine you're seated, along with several other people, at a round table with a globe of the world I the center of it. I think you'll agree that everyone sitting there, from their particular position, would see the globe a little differently. Your view would be slightly different from the person sitting next to you. His view is a little different from the person next to him and so forth. Of course the person sitting directly across the table, even though he is looking at the same globe, will have a completely different perspective. For example, if you're looking at the United States, he will be looking at China.

Then, if you were to ask each person to explain what he saw, you'd obviously get a lot of different answers. But if you put all those answers together and analyzed them, you'd have a pretty accurate description of the earth.

Life is a little like that. We can all look at the same thing and still see it differently. What we see, or our sense of what we see, is usually distorted and influenced by our life experiences. By that, I mean everything we've experienced from infancy to the present, which includes our likes, dislikes, personal preferences, religion, education, and so forth. All of these factors play a role in how we interpret everything. To simplify it, you might say, as far as our life experiences go, we all sit in different seats, resulting in a somewhat different outlook.

Perhaps, that's why several people, with their multitude of experiences and viewpoints, working together in a spirit of cooperation and harmony, will almost always come up with a more comprehensive and realistic plan or solution, than one person could. To reinforce this theory, I would like to paraphrase an old adage and say, "A few heads are better than one!"

The Kernel

After Jim told one of his corny jokes his sister Marianne would inevitably say, "He's popp'n corn again!"

This past week, after Jim's wife, told Marianne's son, Steve, what his mom would always say, he replied, "Yeah, but he's the best corn popper I've ever met!"

Not missing a beat, Jim chimed in, "Maybe that's why they call me the "Kernel!"

A Dick Theory

Not all dicks are guys!

No A O'

Saint Patrick's Day it was indeed, when after a few jars of green beer, at the local pub, Seamus met a fellow Irishman named Connor. "I know a few O'Connors," Seamus said proudly, "but you're the first Connor I ever met. What happened to your O?"

"Beats me," Connor answered. "It was dropped somewhere along the line."

"Well, Seamus replied, after taking a big slug of his green brew (in Saint Patrick's honor, of course), and grinning like a leprechaun dancing the jig. "At least by spelling your name that way, nobody's ever going to call you an ass O!"

Put Words in my Mouth, Please!

It seems strange that the writer's strike has put the late night comedians out of business. This makes it apparent, at least to me, that the writers must put most, if not all the words into the comedians' mouths. Can't they think for themselves? Here I thought, erroneously no doubt, that they were clever fellows who created most of their own material.

The Gene

Women seem to have a spending gene!

Anonymous

Roots

Blondes got roots!

Adios, Sucker

The two things women need from men are sperm and money.

When they no longer need sperm, and the money

goes out the window, they go out the door!

Anonymous

No Time

Clock-watchers have no time for success!

The Rear View

If a lot of the people who wear thongs, could see their
rear view in a mirror, they'd cover their back up!

Definition

Young love: the act of thinking with one's heart
instead of one's head!

Don't Look!

When Brian told Janine that a well-known couple, who badly
wanted children, was having a hard time conceiving, she commented,
"Gosh, all I had to do was to look at it and I got pregnant!"

"In that case," Brian quipped, "I'm not going to show it to you!"

Not His Doctor!

Who do you really think the average guy will
call if he has an erection lasting over four hours?

Heaven on Earth

A good home is about as close as
you're going to get to heaven on earth!

SAT Down

University admission officers that base their selection criteria more on SAT scores than academic performance, should be SAT down and required to take a course in "The Realities of Accomplishment and Success," where the only thing that truly counts is "performance."

Wise Words

Don't live your circumstances, live your potential!

Alex Monteith

The Tell Tale Smell

If you smell bleach, there's probably a blonde around!

And now, folks, the grand finale.

Hold the applause, please!

Less Painful

My life would have been a lot less painful,

if I had learned to land on my feet,

instead of falling on my ass!

Joseph E. Schindler

1932-1999

"My Big Brother and Hero"

During the Great Depression, in March of 1938, almost exactly sixty-one years ago, Joe and I, along with our other two brothers, Gene and Louie, and our sisters, Estella and Francis, were taken to St. Vincent's Villa, the Catholic orphanage in Fort Wayne, Indiana. I can still remember that day; I was only three years old and Joe was five. Joe was crying and wouldn't leave our mother. So she, along with the help of a nun, carried him kicking and screaming into the orphanage. During this time, I was holding on to my mother's skirt and I wasn't crying, not because I was braver, but being younger, I didn't yet realize what he instinctively knew: that we were going to be left there.

When Joe was a kid, he wet the bed. I think that I can mention this without embarrassing him or his family, because as he got older, he talked about it. In the nineteen thirties and early forties, the thinking was that if you wet the bed, you were just too lazy to get up and go to the bathroom. As a result, the nuns at the orphanage were not very nice to the bed wetters. I think they honestly believed that if they embarrassed or punished them, they would quit. Consequently, they would make them take ice-cold baths, or stand with their pissy sheets over their heads in the hallway, where many of the kids would make fun of them or call them fish. I remember how bad I would feel for Joe, but just think how he must have felt!

On St. Nicholas Day, all the kids would get a gingerbread cookie, which was about six inches long and shaped like a man with a face and jacket made out of frosting. That is, all the kids except the ones who had wet the bed the night before! I know that doesn't sound like a big deal, but it was probably the only cookie we got all year and we all really looked forward to it.

Each night we went to bed at ten o'clock and anyone caught up after that would be in big trouble. (At this time I believe I was in the second and Joe in the fourth grade.) So we had a plan. On the night before St. Nicholas Day (which is in November), about an hour after we went to bed, when Joe thought everyone was asleep, he would silently sneak over to my bed, wake me up, and we would go into one of the stalls in the bathroom and huddle together on the floor. There he would read me stories to keep us awake all night so he wouldn't wet the bed, and he would get a gingerbread cookie. (To conserve energy and save money, the heat was turned off about eleven o'clock each night and wouldn't be turned back on until six in the morning, so it got quite chilly.) Then about an hour or so before it was time to get up, and we could hardly keep our eyes open anymore, we would sneak back to bed.

At six o'clock, when the nun came in and clapped her hands to get us up, I ran over to Joe's bed to see how happy he'd be, but I could tell by the look on his face that something was wrong. He had wet the bed! I couldn't believe it! But he told me that he couldn't help it and didn't even know he did it. I believed him. I felt so sorry for him that I gave him half of my gingerbread cookie; but I have to confess, I kept the biggest half.

One day in 1944, when he was twelve, Joe decided to run away. He took off with a buddy and they walked to Huntington, about twenty five miles away, to where his friend's parents lived. They were very poor and either didn't have anything to give them to eat or just didn't want them around, because they left with empty stomachs. By now, they were so hungry that they decided to walk back to the orphanage so they could get a warm meal. Joe told me that all they had to eat during this time were some green apples that they picked, in a farmer's field, on their walk back to Fort Wayne.

In the summer of 1945, Joe and I, along with our sister Bancy (Frances), were taken out of the orphan's home. (I had just finished the fifth grade and Joe the seventh.) We were sent to live with our dad in Elyria, Ohio. Our father was an alcoholic and lived in a shack, probably about twenty by twenty, in a rundown industrial area. He was always gone, and many days we had very little if anything to eat. I remember once all there was, was some sugar and chocolate, so Bancy made fudge and we survived on that for a few days.

Many years later, when Joe and I were working together doing dry wall, we stopped at the Dutch Mill in Bluffton, for lunch. Joe loved the Dutch Mill. He ordered a couple of double burgers, large fries, and I don't know what else. I said to him, "Joe, it's not good for you to eat all that stuff."

"When I was a kid," he answered, "I never had enough to eat, and I'm not going to go hungry again!"

Bancy, being two years older than Joe, really looked out for us. At the orphan's home, Joe and I lived on the first floor and Bancy lived on the fourth floor in the same building. If she heard one of us crying (somehow she could always tell when it was Joe or me), she'd run down the stairs and go after whoever hit us, with her fists flying as wildly as her red hair, no matter how big the guy was.

Somehow, the welfare department found out about our circumstances at our dad's. We were there only a couple of months when they took us and put Joe and me on a farm, and sent Bancy to a different foster home. That farmer didn't want us because he loved kids; he needed someone to do the work. What a deal! It was better than slavery. Not only did he get free labor, he got paid (by the welfare system) to keep us!

We would get up early every morning, feed and milk twenty to thirty cows, feed the pigs and chickens, and when we finished the chores, we would wash up, eat, and then go to school. After school, it was the same all over, in addition to gathering eggs, cleaning out the barn, and whatever else needed to be done. By the time we finished, it was time for bed. We did this every day, and on Saturday, there were extra chores to do.

We didn't think that we had it too bad; we thought everyone worked like that. What we soon found out was that the farmer had a mean streak. He had a rubber hose about eighteen inches long, one of those real heavy ones like they used to make back in the 1940s. If Joe did something that the farmer didn't like, he would beat him with that hose, and every time he hit him, it would leave a black-and-blue mark on his back the size and shape of that hose. The next day, almost Joe's entire back would be black and blue.

Later, when we were alone in our room, we would talk and I'd try to make him feel better. We felt that the only ones in the world that we could count on were each other. When I got beaten, Joe would comfort me and I knew that I could lean on him. I can't speak for him, but I know that I could have never made it through those times without him. To me, Joe will always be "My Big Brother and Hero."

After two and a half years, the welfare department found out what that farmer was doing to us, so they took us and put us in a foster home in Decatur, Indiana. In the next few years, Joe finished high school and joined the air force. By this time he had a chip on his shoulder and, taking into consideration what he had gone through, it was understandable. I never knew him to go out looking for trouble, but if someone pushed him too hard or tried to shove him around, he just wouldn't take it anymore.

Fortunately, about this time, Joe met Janet and she was just what he needed. Under her influence, you could see him gradually settle down and together they raised a nice family of five children.

There were three things that Joe really loved. First was Janet and his family, second the Kansas City Chiefs, and third, he loved his motorcycle. One day, when he was in the air force, in Ipswich, England, the town just outside his base, he jumped on his motorcycle, gave it a kick start, put it in gear, and took off with the throttle wide open. The front wheel lifted off the ground, the back tire spun, and I mean he was off. Well, almost! About a block down, right in the middle of the street, stood a bobby, an English cop, waving his arms for him to stop. When Joe did, the bobby approached him and said, "That was tremendous acceleration!" then proceeded to give him a ticket.

Another time, Joe had just gotten a new motorcycle. I think that it was a Yamaha V-Max, the fastest production motorcycle made at that time. I believe that it would clock around 150 miles per hour. Anyway, he was going to take a friend, Jimmy D'Angelo, for a ride. Now Jimmy just had a bypass operation a few weeks before and Bancy, our sister, told Joe to take it easy. Needless to say, off they went and in a few minutes Joe poked Jimmy to get him to look at the speedometer. They were going a 120. But to Joe, he was taking it easy; after all, the damn thing would go a 150! As far as I know, that was the last motorcycle ride that Jimmy D ever took.

Even after Joe's bad accident on his motorcycle, he still wouldn't give it up. It was just a few weeks ago when he told me he couldn't wait for it to get warmer so he could get his bike out.

How he loved the Kansas City Chiefs! He had a Chiefs license plate, a Chiefs hat, a Chiefs coat, and I don't even want to know what else he had with 'Kansas City Chiefs' on it. I believe that it was Suzi, his daughter, who wrote Len Dawson, the KC quarterback and a Hall of Famer. Len answered her letter and sent her an autographed picture. Joe was sure proud of that.

He would often ask me, "Do you know who's playing tonight?" Or, "Do you know who's on *Monday Night Football*?" Then he would tell me all the details. He would tell me much more than I ever wanted to know about the Kansas City Chiefs. They were, as he would say, "My Boys." Sometimes, he would drive to Effingham, Illinois, to his son Steve's house to watch a Chiefs game on TV, if the game wasn't televised here.

But what he really loved was Janet and his kids. Over the past few years since his retirement, at least three or more days a week, he would sit at my kitchen table and talk to my wife, Fry, or me. He would tell us all about Suzi or Juli, or what the boys, Joey, Steve, or John, were doing and about his grandkids. You could just tell how proud he was of all of them and how much he loved them.

If he heard that his kids or a friend was having a bad time, he would sit there with big tears in his eyes and sometimes even break down and sob. Many people thought that he was rough and tough, but to us who really knew him, he was just a big teddy bear.

But, the love of his life was Janet. Two or three years ago, he told Fry and me how lucky he was to have her and how much she meant to him. Then a few weeks ago, he told us again, and I will quote him as closely as I can; he said, "Janet is the best thing that ever happened to me. I don't know what I would have done without her." Janet, I want you to know that I think so, too. Thank you for bringing out the best in him. Thank you for taking care of him, and thank you for loving him.

Did you know that there are no perfect people in heaven? That's because there are no perfect people. We all have said and done things that we shouldn't have. We might say that we've made mistakes, but according to the Bible, we sinned. However, I honestly believe that no matter what we've done, God will forgive us if we are truly sorry. I also think that when we are born, God deals us a hand, kind of like in cards. Some people get great hands (like being born super rich or talented), some good hands (born to rich or educated parents), some mediocre hands (born into an average family), and some lousy hands (the poor and disadvantaged). Then God sits back and watches how we play those hands. I know that Joe didn't get dealt a very good hand, but he did a great job with the one he got. He raised a beautiful family, treated his fellow man well, was law abiding, and worked hard. Yes, Joe was truly one of the good guys!

When he reached the pearly gates early last Friday morning, I know that Saint Peter didn't ask, "What church did you go to?" And I know that he didn't ask, "Did you go every Sunday?" But, I'll bet that he did ask, "What kind of a life did you live?" And, "How did your treat your fellow man?" And when he pulled out Joe's record and saw how well he played the difficult hand that he was dealt, I'll bet he said, "Come on in, Joe; you've earned a special place in heaven for the exceptional job that you've done and for all you've been through."

And, I can see Joe up there now. I'll bet that he's got the fastest motorcycle in heaven, and I can just picture him trying to get Saint Peter to take a ride so he can scare the hell out of him. And just think: Now he can look down on all the Kansas City Chiefs games and have the best seat in the house, for free!!! And I believe that he's watching us this very minute, with a big smile on his face, because he knows how much Janet and his kids truly appreciated him and how much they and all of us really loved him. God bless you, Joe, and God bless us, because we're sure going to miss you!

Eulogy for

Joseph E. Schindler

March 29, 1999

As written and delivered by his brother,

James A. Schindler

Author's Note

All the stories, in this book, just as in my first book, *Schindler's Tiny Tales & Whatnot,* are as I remember them or as told to me by my family, friends, and acquaintances. Although I might have embellished some for effect, to the best of my knowledge they're all true. As for the *Uncommon Sense* essays and remarks, I plead guilty! Mea culpa!

To all of you who spent your hard-earned dollars and valuable time to buy and read *Schindler's Short Stories & Uncommon Sense,* I compliment you on your impeccable literary taste. Just don't forget to tell your friends how much you liked it! For a book without readers is a little bit like a play without an audience. So, please, don't let me go audienceless! Thanks a million, and Godspeed!